"This book is a rare and personal look into the life and career of one of America's preeminent leaders—with poignant reflections and perspectives on what matters in life. And it comes at an important time in our country. Valuable and timely lessons for all of us. In a series of amazingly honest and human stories, General Dempsey shows us among other things why character really matters."

—CHUCK HAGEL, former secretary of defense, former U.S. senator, and Vietnam veteran

"Real leadership is not a natural gift, a birthright, or even an accident of fate. It is a choice. It is a conscious decision by an all-too-human individual to live to a standard of values and commitment to others that is simultaneously a crushing burden and an elevated calling. Few leaders reflect or understand this genuine, even-when-it-hurts leadership better than General Marty Dempsey. *No Time for Spectators* is a brilliantly clear reflection of what really matters by a leader who lived it."

—STANLEY MCCHRYSTAL, general (ret.), U.S. Army; founder, McChrystal Group; and best-selling author of *Team of Teams*

"Through compelling storytelling, Martin Dempsey shows us the true definition of leadership. Real impact can only be made through action—and *No Time for Spectators* is the clarion call for those yearning to solve the world's complex problems."

—MELLODY HOBSON, co-CEO and president, Ariel Investments

"There's no one I enjoy talking with more about leadership than General Marty Dempsey, and *No Time for Spectators* is the next best thing. If you've ever wondered what more you can do to be a productive, valued member of a team, in any walk of life, I suggest you read this book."

—ADAM SILVER, commissioner, National Basketball Association

"If you're going to learn leadership from anyone, it should be Marty Dempsey! In my 37 years of service, I found no better leader and no finer man. *No Time for Spectators* is the best book you will ever read about how to make tough decisions in challenging times and, more importantly, how to build loyalty from the men and women you lead."

—WILLIAM MCRAVEN, admiral (ret.), U.S. Navy; former chancellor, University of Texas; and best-selling author of *Make Your Bed*

"I have met no one who has thought more deeply about the many dimensions of effective leadership. General Marty Dempsey gleans from the rich experiences of his life insightful and urgently needed lessons about successful leadership, and reminds us of its pivotal importance in any organization or endeavor."

—FATHER JOHN JENKINS, president, University of Notre Dame

"General Marty Dempsey has authored the right message at the right time. *No Time for Spectators* illuminates how leading with character and grace creates an environment in which all can thrive. A thoughtful and dedicated champion of women in the military and in sports, his inspiring stories provide something for anyone who wants to be a better person and leader."

—DAWN STALEY, head coach, women's basketball, University of South Carolina

"A timely memoir and playbook calling for positive action instead of static reaction. Told with humanity, integrity and humor, *No Time for Spectators* is a must-read for leaders, leaders in the making, and those who do not yet realize that they are leaders!"
—Doug Lowey, CEO and founding partner, Brownstone
  Investment Group

"These stories from a good friend and impressive leader both inspire and motivate. *No Time for Spectators* is a must for your 'Final Four' reading list this year!"
—Mike Krzyzewski, head coach, men's basketball, Duke University

"When Marty Dempsey talks about his experiences and the lessons he's taken from them, I listen. His gripping stories make you feel like you were right there with him. In today's leadership environment, his voice and insights are more vital than ever. If you care about your country or care about your company, read this book."
—Ori Brafman, best-selling author of *The Starfish and the Spider*
  and *Radical Inclusion*

"*No Time for Spectators* is what this country and our world hunger for today—a persuasive reminder that loyalty and character matter, that we should live a 'felt life' and not race through the important moments, and that we all need a strong support system. General Dempsey's charisma, compassion, and character leap from these pages and into your heart. You will be a better leader, and a better person, for having had this conversation with one of America's great leaders."
—Bonnie Carroll, founder and president, Tragedy Assistance
  Program for Survivors (TAPS) and 2015 recipient of Presidential
  Medal of Freedom

"I know of no person with better perspective, experience, education, and humble wisdom on the subject of leadership than General Martin Dempsey. He will tell us he doesn't have all the answers, but in his latest book, *No Time for Spectators*, Dempsey makes us ask ourselves all the right questions. Given his depth of knowledge, selfless service, and noble heart, his book leads us to the right answers. Martin Dempsey is a national treasure."

—JAY BILAS, analyst, ESPN

"General Dempsey brings a wealth of timely lessons for ordinary life from his own extraordinary experiences. His compelling story reminds us all of the choices we can make, every day, to engage thoughtfully rather than retreat, to step up when inclined to stand by, reach out when extended a hand, and pause to reflect when hurried along."

—VINCENT PRICE, president, Duke University

"Having the honor to work alongside General Dempsey with USA Basketball has offered me an incredible opportunity to learn from one of the nation's great leaders. In *No Time for Spectators*, General Dempsey's wisdom and humility come through on every page. I can think of no better guide on the path to becoming a better leader—and follower—than General Dempsey."

—JAY WRIGHT, head coach, men's basketball, Villanova University

"I doubt you can find an individual more qualified than Martin Dempsey to give advice on how to lead a life that matters. *No Time for Spectators* is a great reflection from a man with a warrior's heart, an immigrant's spirit, and a servant's soul."
—BILL KRAUSE, former COO, Under Armour, and founder, Mission BBQ

"In fractured times, where more of us lurk fearfully on the sidelines, strong and capable leadership is critical. With his signature gift for storytelling, General Martin Dempsey skillfully outlines what to expect of our leaders, and ourselves, using personal moments from his own accomplished life of service and commitment. *No Time for Spectators* is a timely and timeless playbook about the attributes of loyalty, character, curiosity, skepticism, clarity and yes, responsible rebelliousness. Whether you are CEO of a corporation or of your family, this wisdom will help all of us rise to the challenges presented in today's complex world."
—BOB and LEE WOODRUFF, founders, Bob Woodruff Foundation

NO TIME FOR
SPECTATORS

THE LESSONS THAT MATTERED MOST
FROM WEST POINT TO THE WEST WING

MARTIN E. DEMPSEY

18TH CHAIRMAN OF THE JOINT CHIEFS OF STAFF

NO TIME FOR SPECTATORS

The Lessons That Mattered Most From West Point To The West Wing

Copyright © 2020 by Martin Dempsey

Published by Missionday

Hardcover ISBN: 978-1-939714-21-3
Ebook ISBN: 978-1-939714-22-0
Library of Congress Control Number: 2020932948

Cover design by Domini Dragoone
Interior design and production by Domini Dragoone
Cover photo by Myles Cullen, DoD
Author photo © Saskia Potter

Printed in the United States of America
Distributed by Publishers Group West

First Printing 2020
10 9 8 7 6 5 4 3 2 1

To Deanie,
who's been there every step of the way.

CONTENTS

AUTHOR'S NOTE

The events in this book are recounted as I remember them. Any inaccuracies are a result of the passage of time or the ever-present "fog of war" as events unfolded. I am confident that the stories and the conversations that bring them to life in this book accurately capture the spirit of the moment.

INTRODUCTION

I could barely keep my eyes open. And looking around at my classmates in the West Point class of 1974, I saw that I was not alone. On this hot August day, the auditorium was more like a master bedroom than a lecture hall. We were plebes—freshman cadets—lower in the hierarchy than the superintendent's dog or the commandant's cat. Or so we had been told.

In this audience were individuals who would become giants of industry, highly successful doctors, lawyers, astronauts, diplomats, senior government officials, and, of course, military leaders. But we didn't know that now. In this moment, we were simply united in our effort to stay awake or suffer the consequences: being tapped on the shoulder by some faculty member patrolling the aisles of this English lecture.

The lecturer was known to me only by name. As plebes, we had to memorize the names of all the department heads. This one was Colonel John Sutherland. I studied the rows of ribbons on his chest, not really knowing what any of them meant. I also studied his handlebar mustache. *I'll be able to remember that if I'm quizzed on the department heads,* I thought.

"And so, class of 1974, I welcome you to the Department of English," I heard him say.

Sounds like he's finishing up, I thought hopefully.

"As you journey through your four years at West Point, and as you begin your professional lives afterward in the service of your country, I wish you the quality of a felt life." He was finished.

What was that last thing he said? It sounded important, and I wanted to remember it. *A felt life? I wonder what that means.* I didn't know it at the time, but that question would be a lifetime in the answering and make a real difference in the way I learned to lead and to follow.

"On your feet, bean heads," an upperclassman barked.

With that, we were ushered to our next introductory lecture.

I didn't want to go to West Point.

In early 1970, as I began my last semester at John S. Burke Catholic High School, I had what I thought was a pretty good plan in place for my future. I had been accepted to Manhattan College in New York City and intended to follow a prelaw curriculum. I had been awarded a New York State Regents scholarship, and it seemed likely that the school would provide a modest track-and-field scholarship as well. So the finances of a quality college education were in place. And for about a year I had been dating Deanie Sullivan, a young lady two years behind me who would eventually become my wife. Even then she seemed to me to be "the one." She was cute, smart, and athletic. I didn't want to get ahead of myself, but things did seem to be falling into place nicely.

Over Christmas, my uncle Jack had thrown me a bit of a curveball, encouraging me to apply for an appointment to the U.S. Naval Academy. Uncle Jack was a World War II Navy veteran, and though I had no real interest in pursuing a career in the Navy, out of respect for him I'd gone ahead and submitted the application.

In early February, I received a letter from the Naval Academy instructing me to report to the nearest military installation for a medical examination and physical fitness test. Since we were living in Greenwood Lake, New York, at the time, that meant West Point.

When I showed up on the appointed day, I already knew my way around West Point pretty well, because my friends and I often attended sporting events on campus. But I knew next to nothing about what went on there.

The medical examination was first, and it was uneventful. Except for astigmatism in my left eye, I was healthy.

As I walked from the hospital to the cadet gymnasium for the physical fitness test, I took note of how bitterly cold and perpetually overcast West Point was. The cadets I saw along the way were bundled in heavy gray wool overcoats and hunched against the wind howling off the Hudson River. *Can't imagine four years of that,* I thought.

"Gentlemen," the imposing physical fitness instructor began, "today you will be tested on five events. These events will test your strength, your agility, and your stamina. Do your best on them. Physical fitness is an important part of our overall evaluation of you."

I performed slightly above average in the first three events: chin-ups, a standing broad jump, and a kneeling basketball throw. Next came sit-ups, and I pushed myself to a maximum score. Although I really had no intention of going to Annapolis, the competitor in me had taken over.

The last event was a three-hundred-meter shuttle run. It required us to shuttle small wooden blocks placed twenty-five meters apart back and forth on a basketball court, making twelve trips to displace the blocks from end to end as fast as possible. The previous spring I had won the county four-hundred-meter championship, held on West Point's outdoor track, so I was excited to see how I could do in this event.

When I completed the event, the physical fitness instructor approached me.

"Mr. Dempsey. That was impressive. Would you mind staying behind for a moment? There's someone I'd like you to meet."

"Sure," I replied. He disappeared through a door at the far end of the court.

About ten minutes later he reappeared, accompanied by a man I recognized. It was Carleton Crowell, Army's track and field coach since 1951.

"Hello, sir," I said, extending my hand. "I'm Marty Dempsey."

"Hello, Marty." He shook my hand. "I'm told that you nearly set a record in our three-hundred-meter shuttle run. I don't think we've met, but didn't I see you up here for a high school track meet recently?"

"Yes, sir. I run for Burke Catholic."

"That's right. Well, are you coming to West Point?"

"No, sir. I'm actually completing the requirements for an appointment to Navy."

"That so?" he said. "Well, if that doesn't work out for you, would you consider coming here, assuming you're qualified?"

Not really, I thought. But I knew that wouldn't be the polite thing to say.

"Yes, sir," I replied.

"Good. I'll start a file on you, and if you give us access to your application to Navy, we'll take it from there. Hope we see you again."

With that, he turned and walked away, and I made my way out of the gym and headed home. I told my parents about meeting the track coach, but I didn't give it much thought beyond that.

Two months later, in early April, I received notice in the mail that I had been rejected by the Naval Academy because of my vision. In the days before Lasik eye surgery, 50 percent of each class entering the

Naval Academy had to have perfect vision, so that when they graduated four years later, the Academy could meet its quota for naval aviators. Though it's never fun to be rejected for anything, I honestly wasn't disappointed.

The spring became summer. After graduating from high school on June 22, I was poised to make the summer of 1970 a memorable one.

To jump-start the season, on June 27 Deanie and I made a day trip to the Jersey Shore, just a couple of hours away. We returned at about 6:00 P.M. to find Deanie's mother standing in the driveway.

"Marty," she said, "your mom has been trying to reach you. She seems pretty excited about something. Why don't you call her from here before you head home?"

This was, of course, before cell phones, so there had been no way for my mother to reach me at the beach. I dialed on Deanie's family's landline, and my mom picked up almost immediately.

"Marty, we need you to come home right away," she said excitedly. "We received a Western Union telegram today notifying you that you've received an appointment to West Point. You're to report on July 1, and there are some things you've got to get done between then and now."

"Well, I'll come right home, Mom. But there's no way I'm going to West Point—especially not four days from now."

My mind flashed back to my conversation with the track coach. Someone who had received an appointment must have changed their mind at the very last moment, and I had been selected from the alternate list. *Probably shouldn't have been so polite,* I thought.

"Just come home so we can talk about it, okay?" my mother said.

"Sure, Mom. I'll be home in about forty-five minutes."

Back outside, I told Deanie and her mother what had just happened. They were as surprised by the news as I had been. Deanie was speechless.

"Don't worry," I told her. "I'm not going to West Point. I'll talk to you tomorrow."

Forty-five minutes later, I was sitting at home in the kitchen with my parents. I could see my two brothers and two sisters sitting in the living room. They were pretending to watch television, but I knew they were actually eavesdropping to hear what was going to happen. I had no doubts: I wasn't going to West Point. My mother started the conversation.

"Marty, this is such an unbelievable opportunity . . ."

Moe and Sarah Dempsey grew up in Bayonne, New Jersey, each the child of two Irish immigrants. They married in their early twenties and lived on the ground floor of a small two-story house owned by my maternal grandmother, who had purchased it when she became a widow in her early forties. They both worked—they had to in order to "make ends meet," as they described their persistent and often overwhelming financial challenges while I was growing up. My father was a warehouseman at the Esso Oil refinery in Bayonne, and my mother stocked shelves at a store in Jersey City. Throughout their married lives, they sacrificed everything to provide opportunities for their five children.

I knew that my mother, a devout Catholic, was convinced that this telegram from West Point was divine intervention.

The next thirty minutes were a blur. My mother first came at me with logic, then invoked fate, then appealed to my sense of responsibility. I was holding my own, countering each parry with well-articulated arguments.

And then my mother began to cry.

Oh my God, I thought. *I'm going to West Point.*

I continued to put up a decent fight, but I knew I was on the defensive. My dad was a little more sympathetic to my reluctance. An avid consumer of news, he knew that the war in Vietnam was going badly and becoming increasingly unpopular. My siblings weighed in at one point, arguing that I should be allowed to do what I wanted to do. We were children of the sixties, after all.

But eventually I succumbed, telling my mother that I would give West Point a try for the summer and then leave in time to make it to Manhattan College for the fall semester.

The next day I told Deanie the same thing.

Three days after that, on July 1, 1970, I put on an Army uniform for the first time. I wouldn't take it off for the last time until forty-five years later.

There are people in our lives who may know more about what's good for us than we do.

I thought I should end my Army career.

When Deanie and I married in 1976, I assured her that once I had completed the five-year service obligation for my West Point education, I would resign from the Army and pursue a more stable career in civilian life. The prospect of a career of frequent and sometimes unpredictable moves and family separations seemed too daunting, and neither of us knew enough about the Army to make a long-term decision at that point.

By the time I completed my five-year commitment, I realized that I liked the Army. Deanie liked it too, but we had a one-year-old and a second child on the way, so it was still hard to think about committing to the Army long term.

As a result, we "negotiated" each successive assignment, with me mostly on the side of continuing to serve and Deanie mostly encouraging me to at least think about another career.

Then an interesting thing happened. In the mid-nineties, as I completed my twentieth year of service and was selected for promotion to colonel, we reversed roles. I began to think seriously about transitioning to a second career, while Deanie—and the kids—became advocates for continued military service.

My deployment to Operation Desert Storm in 1991 had been hard on all of us. When the Spearhead Division was called to duty in Saudi Arabia and then Iraq, we left our families in Germany, not sure when we'd be back. In those days, our only reliable contact was by letter, and it usually took two weeks or more for letters to make their way to and from our bases in Germany.

Chris, Megan, and Caity were thirteen, twelve, and eight that year. Deanie had done a terrific job getting our own family—and helping other families—through the deployment. However, as the kids approached high school, and as it became clear that my increasing seniority would require even more frequent moves, I began to feel guilty about the hardships that my chosen career seemed sure to impose on my family.

But I hadn't realized that my career had become their career too.

When I was promoted to colonel, I knew I would soon be considered for brigade command and, if selected, we would have to move. We were living in Fairfax, Virginia, a great assignment for the family. The two older kids were thriving at Fairfax High School. Chris had started high school in Germany; now he was a junior and Megan was a sophomore. A move at that point would almost certainly mean three different high schools in four years for them.

One evening, after the went kids to bed, I told Deanie I had made a decision.

"I've decided to decline brigade command."

I expected that my proclamation would be greeted warmly. Not so much.

"What are you talking about?" she said.

"I'm going to decline command. That way, we'll be able to stay here long enough for the kids to finish high school," I replied, awaiting the appreciation that would surely follow my obvious concern for our children.

"But if you decline command, that's the end of your career, right?"

"Pretty much. I'll probably be able to do a couple of years in the Pentagon, but then I'll have to retire."

"Then why would you do that?"

This isn't going as I expected, I thought.

"Well, I've got twenty-one years under my belt. There are lots of military-friendly businesses in this area. I'll start looking around for a job, and we can stay here for the kids to complete high school."

I can't believe I'm still not getting through about the high school thing, I thought.

"Don't you think we should talk about this?" she asked.

"That's what I thought we were doing," I responded defensively.

"No, I mean with the kids."

"We can," I said, "but I just assumed that you'd be happier staying here and that they'd be happier staying at Fairfax High."

"Well, I do like it here, but I've liked a lot of other places too. I love the people we've met, the adventures we've shared, and the satisfaction of helping military families along the way. As for the kids, don't forget that they've also been on this journey with you their whole lives. I think you should get their input before you make such a big decision."

I hate it when she's right, I thought.

Two days later, everyone made it home in time for dinner. After asking the kids how their day had gone, I told them about my decision to decline command and retire. They all stopped eating and stared at me incredulously.

My child of few words spoke first. "That's ridiculous," Chris said.

My analytical child spoke second. "Really, Dad, why would you do that?" Megan added.

My emotional child spoke last. "That just makes me sad," Caity said. Deanie just smiled.

The kids went on to explain that they had loved growing up in the Army. They reminded me that there were a lot of young soldiers and junior leaders and their families we had served with who would be disappointed if their mom and I left the Army. They said they didn't know a lot about what would come next in my career, but they were certain the Army would be better with us in it. They finished by assuring me that they would do fine if we had to move again.

Obviously, I didn't decline command, and I did continue to serve—for more than twenty more years from that day.

There are people in our lives who may know more about what's good for us than we do.

I thought my Army career would be ended.

In December 2008 I was promoted to four-star general and placed in command of the Army's Training and Doctrine Command (TRADOC). It was a great job that involved developing and overseeing the training and education of the entire Army, from basic training for new recruits through the Army War College for senior colonels. Our motto was "Victory Starts Here!" and it felt like it.

The Army has dozens of training bases across the country, so there was a lot of travel involved. In June 2010 I had just returned to my headquarters in Fort Monroe, Virginia, after a lengthy trip to the Midwest, when I noticed a lump on the left side of my neck, just under the jaw.

Must have caught some kind of infection during my travels, I thought.

Then came a persistent sore throat, and the lump wasn't going away. Concerned, I scheduled an appointment with our local military doctor.

"It's unusual," he said, "but you're in pretty good shape, and no other risk factors are present. I'll give you a Z-Pak, and we'll see if that takes care of it." He did. It didn't.

Two weeks later I was back in his office.

"Could be dental," he said. "Let's schedule an appointment up at Fort Eustis with a dentist." We did. It wasn't.

Two weeks later I was in his office a third time.

"Okay, time to get more aggressive with our diagnosis," he told me. "I'll schedule an appointment with an ear, nose, and throat specialist up at Fort Eustis." I was traveling overseas to Iraq and Afghanistan, so the appointment was scheduled for three weeks later.

By the time the appointment came, I could think of little else. They took several X-rays of my throat and looked through a tube inserted into my throat through my nose.

"What do you think, Doc?" I asked nervously.

"I think you should go up to Walter Reed for an MRI. It could be nothing, but I see an area that gives me some concern. Let's make sure we know what's going on," he replied.

"Could it be cancer, Doc?"

"I don't think so, but we need to be sure."

Now I was really nervous. Work was a welcome distraction, but I awoke each morning wondering if I had cancer. Anyone who has had a cancer scare, or the actual disease, will tell you that time slows, and it's hard to focus on anything else.

Deanie and I met with a specialist at Walter Reed Army Hospital in Bethesda, Maryland. He sent me through the maze of corridors for an MRI, then to another part of the hospital for a "fine needle aspiration" of the lump on my neck. It was a biopsy, and there was nothing fine about it. Back to see the doctor in his office.

"What do you think, Doc?" I asked.

"I think you have throat cancer," he said matter-of-factly.

That was pretty blunt, I thought. I could feel fear beginning to encroach on my otherwise very happy life.

"But we won't know for sure until the results of the biopsy come back," he informed me.

"How long will that take?"

"About a week."

"Okay." Not much else to say.

A week later, I learned that the biopsy had revealed cancerous cells in a saliva gland. The doctor explained that the gland wasn't the primary source of the cancer; it likely originated in a small tumor on the base of my tongue. "Squamous cell carcinoma" was the medical term I would learn to hate.

I was given the option of being treated at Walter Reed or at Naval Medical Center Portsmouth near my headquarters and our home at Fort Monroe, Virginia. Deanie and I both concluded that it would be better to go with Portsmouth, so that I could continue to work as much as possible and live in our own house during treatment.

At my first meeting with the surgeon, he told me that he wanted to schedule a biopsy of the tumor. It would require me to be anesthetized. While I was still under, he would analyze the tissue sample he took. If it was positive for cancer, he would insert a feeding tube into my stomach. A dentist standing by to take part in the procedure would pull all of my molars. All of this was in preparation for the actual cancer treatment, which would include both radiation and chemotherapy.

"That's a lot to process, Doc." He was a great guy, and he could see Deanie and I were a little dazed by it all.

"The treatment will include thirty-five radiation treatments over seven weeks. Every other Monday, you'll receive an infusion of chemotherapy. We'll insert a feeding tube before we start because you're likely to reach a point where, because of the radiation, you won't be able to swallow. At that point, you'll need to feed yourself through the tube. We pull the molars because the radiation will affect the ability of your jaw to fight infection in that area. Better to do these things now than when you're weakened by treatment. The most important thing for you to remember and focus on is that we can beat this. Your radiologist and clinical oncologist are the best."

"Okay." Not much else to say.

Many of my memories of the next three months are a blur, but some are vivid.

One Sunday morning about halfway through my treatment, Deanie and I awoke and began dressing for church. I finished first, went downstairs, and took a seat at the kitchen island to wait for her. We lived only about half a mile from the church, so we routinely walked there. It was a pleasant walk along one of historic Fort Monroe's tree-lined streets.

When she came into the kitchen, I stood—or tried to stand—and found that I couldn't. It was a strange sensation. I couldn't tell if I was too weak to stand or couldn't remember how. All I knew was that I couldn't stand, and I didn't know why.

"Are you okay?" Deanie asked. I just sat there looking and feeling confused.

"I'm not sure," I said. "Well, not really. I can't move." I could see that I was making her nervous. "I'm just feeling really weak right now. Give me a minute."

"I'll get you some water. Maybe you're dehydrated," she said hopefully. "Do you want me to drive us to church this morning?" she asked.

"Well, if I can get up, we can still walk. If I can't get up, I'm not going to be able to get out to the car. Let's give it another few minutes."

"Should we call the doctor?" she asked.

"Not yet." *Probably should,* I thought, *but surely I can muscle through this.* "I'm not in any pain," I told her, even though we both knew pain had nothing to do with the decision. "I just can't move."

A few minutes later I gave it another shot. This time I made it to my feet, but I was unimaginably weak. I felt as though I were carrying some huge weight on my shoulders. The sensation felt like it was beginning to pass, but not fast enough.

"Let's see how far I can get," I said.

Deanie helped steady me down the two stairs at the back door, and we began to walk toward the church. I was moving slowly, very slowly, but we didn't have far to go. Then I felt the weight on my shoulders beginning to return.

What the heck is going on? I thought. *I used to run this distance in less than two minutes, and now I may not make it at all?* I could feel myself getting angry. Not sure at whom or what. Just angry. I couldn't figure it out. It was beyond reason. *Is this what it feels like to be near death?* I wondered. These kinds of thoughts weren't helpful, I knew. I tried to brush them away.

Once inside the church, I slumped into my seat and remained there throughout the service. Several people came over after the Mass to say hello. I apologized for not getting up. Eventually, we were the only ones left in the church. After a while I felt like I was ready to attempt the return trip.

We made it home in about the same time it had taken us to get to church, and I sat down in a chair on our front porch for about an hour.

Then, as suddenly as it had come upon me, the feeling passed. I stood up and walked inside to tell a much-relieved Deanie that I felt better. We agreed we would discuss it with my doctor the next day.

As it turned out, I never had that sensation again. The doctor suggested that it was probably some combination of dehydration and a reaction to the chemotherapy pushing my body to new depths. I was just glad it was gone.

The other memories of this time in my life are more about the process of fighting cancer. Near-constant praying, accompanied by feelings of guilt that I'd never prayed as much when I was healthy. Deanie putting aside her life to be my caregiver at home. Not knowing what to say on phone calls with our children. Persistent nausea. The unforgettable kindness and concern of a particular nurse practitioner.

I managed a full workday for the first third of the treatment and about a half day for the middle third. During the final third, and for about two weeks after the completion of treatment, I couldn't work at all. When I rang the bell in the radiation clinic, signaling the end of treatment, Deanie and I cried. Most everyone does.

It would be another few weeks before a PET scan confirmed that the tumor was gone. It would be another few months before I regained my strength and began to feel like myself again.

Deanie, my medical team at Portsmouth, and my colleagues at TRADOC had pulled me through. It was all a stark and powerful reminder that we accomplish very little in life alone.

There are people in our lives who may know more about what's good for us than we do.

I didn't want to be Chairman of the Joint Chiefs of Staff.

Halfway through my cancer treatment, the Chief of Staff of the Army, General George Casey, flew by helicopter to Fort Monroe to visit our headquarters and check up on me. He came to my quarters and sat across from me at the island in our kitchen. After exchanging pleasantries and expressing support for my fight against cancer, he told me that he had one piece of business he wanted to discuss.

"Sure, sir," I replied. "What's up?"

"The secretary of the Army and I want you to be my successor when I retire in about a year. We want to nominate you to be the next Chief of Staff of the Army."

I stared at him for a moment. I was genuinely and deeply honored to be considered for the job. After more than thirty-six years in the Army, the chance to lead it was something beyond my expectations.

But I had just started to lose significant weight from my cancer treatment. I was just starting to battle real nausea. I was just starting to have the inevitable doubts that I would be able to beat this cancer.

"Sir," I said, "I can't even react to that right now. I am really honored that you have that kind of confidence in me. Not to be dramatic, though, but I'm not even sure I'm going to survive, let alone be healthy enough to be the Chief of Staff of the Army."

"I understand, Marty. I'm not asking for a decision today, but there is a timing issue with the nomination. We'll have to put together a nomination packet, and we'll have to get you over to the White House to be interviewed by President Obama before the packet goes over to Congress. When do you think you would be in a position to let us know and strong enough to meet the president?"

I had no idea when I'd be strong enough to meet the president. I just knew my treatments would be over at the end of October.

"I think I'll be ready by Thanksgiving, sir," I told him. "If you can't wait that long, I completely understand."

"We can wait," he said. "We want you to be the next chief."

After he left, I told Deanie about our conversation. She was as shocked as I was. But we both decided to focus on the task at hand.

When my cancer treatment ended, I expected to begin feeling better immediately. But there are always surprises in cancer treatment, and this was one of them. I actually felt worse for the next two weeks as the residual radiation and chemotherapy continued to work on my body. Nevertheless, by about the third week after treatment, I began to feel better. Thanksgiving was a week away.

On the day before Thanksgiving I called General Casey and told him I would be honored to be Chief of Staff of the Army and that he could schedule the meeting with the president. He asked if I could come up to Washington and meet with President Obama on December 4. I told him I'd be there.

Thanksgiving came and went. More to be thankful for that year than almost any other.

The following Monday, I decided to try on my dress uniform to make sure it was ready for my trip to the White House on Wednesday. I was unsettled by what I saw in the mirror. During cancer treatment, and especially in the past four weeks, I had lost nearly thirty pounds. I looked awful. My face was gaunt, and my uniform hung like a sack from my depleted frame.

Not likely to get the job looking like this, I thought. *Not much I can do about it, though.*

On Wednesday I made my way to the Pentagon and rode to the White House with Admiral Mike Mullen, the Chairman of the Joint

Chiefs of Staff. We took a seat in the waiting room just off the Oval Office. I had been in the Oval before to meet with both President Clinton and President Bush, but it's a very special place, and I could feel the butterflies churning in my stomach.

It wasn't long before the president's receptionist let us know he was ready to see us. As we approached the door to the Oval Office, it swung open and the president emerged. I had never met him. He smiled broadly.

"Hello, Marty," he said. We shook hands. "Thanks for coming to the White House today. I know what you've been going through. We have some personnel decisions coming up, and I asked Secretary Gates and Mike to find time for me to meet you."

"Glad I could make it, sir. Thanks for inviting me," I said.

Was that the right thing to say? I wondered. But this wasn't a time for self-doubt, I reminded myself.

He turned to walk into the Oval Office. I followed him.

Each president redecorates the Oval Office, and I stole a glance around the room to see how President Obama had chosen to furnish it during his time. He noticed my interest in the circular rug that took up two thirds of the office, and he kindly took a moment to explain its significance to me.

Then he took a seat in an armchair across the room from his desk. I sat on a couch facing him. Mike Mullen sat on the other couch facing me. An aide offered me a glass of water, which I gladly accepted. The president leaned forward in his chair.

"Marty," he began, "as I said in the hallway, I'm about to make some personnel decisions about the country's senior military leaders, and I wanted to take a few moments to get to know you. So, if it's okay with you, I'll start with a few questions about our national security."

For the next thirty minutes, President Obama asked me about the national security challenges facing our nation. We talked about China and the Pacific, about Russia and Europe, about Iran and the Middle East, about North Korea. We talked about terrorism and cybersecurity.

At one point, the president asked me what I thought he should expect of his military advisers.

"Well, Mr. President, those advising you on anything better have their facts straight. They better have the courage to tell you the truth, even if they think it may not be what you want to hear. When they present you problems, they better be prepared to recommend solutions. They should present you options, not ultimatums, and be able to articulate the risks associated with each option."

"Interesting," he said. "Anything else?"

"Yes, sir. They should know that you don't have to take their advice, but when you do make a decision based on their advice, you'll own it," I concluded.

He smiled.

"I agree with you, Marty, and I understand that I have certain responsibilities to my advisers too."

Not long after that exchange, the president began to stand up. Admiral Mullen and I did the same. The interview was over. The president walked us to the door, then turned and shook my hand.

"Thanks for coming over, Marty. I'm pretty sure we're going to have the chance to work together in the near future."

As Admiral Mullen and I walked back toward our car, he complimented me on a good office call. I told him I was little curious about why the president hadn't asked me a single question about the Army. Mike just shrugged and suggested that he must have had other things on his mind. Later that day, I returned to my headquarters in Fort Monroe.

About a week later, Secretary of Defense Bob Gates called to tell me that the president had selected me as the next Chief of Staff of the Army. There would be a confirmation hearing scheduled before the Senate Armed Services Committee (SASC) in January, and once confirmed, I would take the job in April.

I thanked him. I had known Secretary Gates since before he became secretary of defense, when he was a member of the Iraq Survey Group assessing our mission in Iraq in 2007. He was very supportive of me during my time as acting commander of U.S. Central Command (CENTCOM), had been instrumental in my becoming TRADOC commander, and was now a strong advocate of my becoming Chief of Staff of the Army.

I was confirmed by the SASC in early February, and Deanie and I began making plans for the move from our house in Fort Monroe to the house in Fort Myer designated for the Chief of Staff of the Army. I selected a transition team to help me prepare for my new role, and Deanie reached out to a great Air Force spouse and talented interior designer, Debbie Biscone, to help her prepare the house that would be our home for the next four years.

We moved into Quarters #1 at Fort Myer in late March. The ceremony making me the thirty-seventh Chief of Staff of the Army was scheduled for April 11. Deanie rushed to prepare the house before our family arrived for the big event. In passing, I jokingly reminded her of the military superstition that you should never hang the last curtain in a military house or it will be time to move again.

She wasn't amused.

On April 12, the day after I became Chief of Staff of the Army, I arrived at the Pentagon eager to begin making my mark on the Army. When I entered the office, my executive officer (XO) handed me the day's schedule. I noticed that my first event of the day was an office call with the secretary of defense. *Must be going to receive my marching orders,* I thought.

It was a short walk from my office around the E-ring of the Pentagon to Secretary Gates's office. I took a seat in his waiting room, and in just a few minutes I was ushered into his office.

Secretary Gates was standing at a window with his hands behind his back, looking out over the Potomac River and the nation's capital. Without turning to me, he told me to have a seat at a small round table a few feet from his massive desk.

That's odd, I thought. Secretary Gates was very personable and in the past had always greeted me warmly. *Surely I haven't done anything yet to cause him to lose confidence in me.*

He turned. "Marty, I'm going to tell you something this morning that's going to make you angry with me," he said.

"Impossible, sir. I wouldn't be here without you. You've always been supportive of me. There's nothing you can say that would make me angry with you," I replied.

"I want you to be the next Chairman of the Joint Chiefs of Staff."

"Except that."

He laughed. I sat stone-faced.

My mind was racing. I knew that the current chairman's tour of duty would end in September. Did he really mean that I would be the Chief of Staff of the Army only for the next five months? From my time working with General Hugh Shelton in the late 1990s, I knew that the chairman is a very public figure who must balance the needs of all the services and those of the combatant commanders around the globe. He is responsible for advising the president and consulting with Congress. Those responsibilities are often competing and usually controversial. I used to joke with Mike Mullen that he had a lot in common with a piñata. Now it seemed like a bad joke.

"You really don't want to be the chairman, do you?" he said.

"No, sir. I don't." *Maybe I can talk him out of it,* I thought hopefully.

"That's why you're the right man for the job," he said.

I guess not.

"Look, sir," I said. "I'm obviously honored to be considered for that job. Being the nation's top military officer and helping the president deal with the many security challenges we face would be truly remarkable. But I think I can really make a difference in the Army, and the Army in particular has some issues after ten years at war."

"You'll be a terrific Chief of Staff of the Army for the next few months, Marty. We had to make you Chief of Staff of the Army before we could nominate you as Chairman of the Joint Chiefs of Staff." (The chairman, I knew, must have served as either a service chief or a combatant commander to be eligible for the position.) "The fact of the matter is, the job we think is most suited for you is chairman."

"Does the president want me to be chairman, sir?" I asked.

"He does, but he wanted me to talk with you about it first."

"Can I discuss this with Deanie, sir?"

"Of course, but only with her."

"Thanks, sir. I trust you know how grateful I am for your support. We've always served wherever we're asked to serve, and this will be no exception. We'd just appreciate a little time to let it sink in."

That night I broke the news to Deanie.

"Can't you just say no?" she asked.

"No. That wouldn't be right."

"I know." She sighed. "I just feel bad that we've been so excited about the chance to help the Army."

"We can still help the Army," I told her. "It's just that we'll also have an opportunity to do our best for the Navy, Air Force, and Marines."

"Well, that part will be rewarding, I guess."

She seemed to be warming a bit to the idea. And then she remembered that we would have to move from the house designated for the

Chief of Staff of the Army to the one designated for the Chairman of the Joint Chiefs of Staff, less than a hundred yards away.

"I can't believe it!" she said, exasperated. "I just finished hanging the curtains."

"I told you not to hang that last one," I reminded her.

She was not amused.

Five and a half months later, I became the eighteenth Chairman of the Joint Chiefs of Staff.

There are people in our lives who may know more about what's good for us than we do.

> ## *This is a book about doing what's right for the right reasons, whether you are called upon to lead or to follow.*

The lessons gathered in these pages could be interpreted simply as a call to "bloom where you're planted." There's something to that, of course, but it oversimplifies something far more important.

This is a book about expectations. It's a book that examines what we should reasonably expect of our leaders and what our leaders should reasonably expect of us. It's an exploration of the attributes necessary to produce men and women of character and consequence, whatever life brings their way.

It's about learning to live a felt life.

This is a book written from a belief that for the good of all of us, each of us should accept that it's *No Time for Spectators.*

Some of the expectations laid out in this book will seem familiar. Others less so. I feel an urgency in advocating them, as it seems clear that for a variety of reasons our interactions in both the public and the private spheres have become more guarded, less candid, too emotional, and too polarized. We are more fearful, more willing to challenge the beliefs of others but less willing to have our own beliefs challenged. The only way we can overcome these trends is to get off the sidelines.

I present these expectations in a way that they've never been presented before—obviously, since I illuminate them with stories from my life. It would be unfortunate, though, if they are dismissed as unique to me because of my success. I've been fortunate, very fortunate, but I believe there is an everyman aspect to much of my good fortune.

Chapter 1 begins at the beginning with a discussion of my strong belief that we should all *learn to follow first.*

Chapter 2 sets the foundation for all that comes after by making the argument that, while we all aspire to win and to succeed at whatever we do, we must not forget that *character matters.*

Chapter 3 asserts that our education must never end, and we should all *encourage passionate curiosity.*

Chapter 4 contends that there are limits to loyalty, and we should all strive to *understand loyalty* better.

Chapter 5 cautions that even though we live in a fast-paced, information-saturated, intensely scrutinized world, it's important that we *don't hurry.*

Chapter 6 suggests that there are *welcome moments of surprising clarity* in each of our lives, and we should rely upon them in making important decisions.

Chapter 7 argues that we actually should *sweat the small stuff*, so that we're prepared when the big stuff comes our way.

Chapter 8 describes how hard it can be to know what's true and makes a case for *sensible skepticism.*

Chapter 9 notes that most positive change starts with a challenge to the status quo and makes a case for *responsible rebelliousness.*

There really is *No Time for Spectators*. The question is what to do about it.

CHAPTER ONE

LEARN TO FOLLOW FIRST

In the past few months, several leaders in very different sectors of our society have expressed to me their growing concern with how relationships are evolving among leaders and followers.

First a U.S. Army drill sergeant—one of those responsible for turning civilian recruits into Army soldiers—lamented that today's young recruits "have very short attention spans, almost to the point of being disrespectful." Then a corporate CEO mused that his young executives are "easily distracted and have difficulty staying with extended tasks." And finally, the commissioner of the National Basketball Association observed that young players frequently "seem unhappy."

I've noticed many of the same things myself. Trying to gain a better understanding of this phenomenon, I've read numerous studies that attribute it to generational differences, concluding that members of recent generations simply share the characteristics of being inattentive, distracted, and unhappy. I've heard arguments that smartphones and social media have made us more connected to the world but also more isolated individually. Some people assert that the sharp edges of our current political atmosphere bleed into our day-to-day interactions and make us trust one another less.

All of these explanations have some merit, but none of them persuade me. Shrugging it all off as a generational inevitability is just too easy. Social media may be a factor, but there's no turning back from the reality of ubiquitous information and intense scrutiny. And politics change—always have and always will—as reasonable people disagree about how to address the complex problems facing us.

Rather, I suggest that all of these issues—inattentiveness, the propensity to be distracted, and unhappiness—hint at a single factor, one that's bigger and more interesting, and that we may actually be able to do something about: young (and not-so-young) men and women, regardless of occupation, status, and affluence, think less and less today about what they should reasonably expect of each other as leaders and followers. They lack a common baseline of expectations.

Particularly neglected is consideration of what it means to be a follower. And that's a question relevant to all of us, whether we're leaders or followers (or both, since almost all leaders also follow someone). Without a common understanding of followership, we feel disoriented in the leader-follower relationship.

In thinking about this conundrum, it seems to me that the best leaders learn how to follow first.

In *Radical Inclusion*, Ori Brafman and I asserted that belonging is the most basic of human instincts. Further, we noted that in an environment of ubiquitous information, intense scrutiny, and rapid change, it is harder for leaders to lead and to create a sense of belonging within their teams. For all of those reasons, I think it's also harder for followers to know how to follow. The result is that fewer of us experience the safety and comfort that comes with a sense of belonging.

Developing a sense of belonging among the individuals in an organization is a shared responsibility among leaders and followers. When that shared responsibility produces a sense of belonging—and its by-product, trust—the organization and its members perform better, are more attentive and less distracted, and feel better about themselves.

What follows are a few personal experiences in learning and teaching how to follow.

THE CLOTHING FORMATION
WEST POINT, 1970

It's nearly the end of the day, I thought thankfully, heading downstairs with my eleven plebe squadmates. It was time to line up in front of the barracks for the last briefing of the day by our upperclassman squad leader. The day had begun at 5:00 A.M., and tomorrow would be more of the same. I was looking forward to getting back upstairs, sitting at my desk for an hour or so polishing my shoes and belt buckle, and then going to bed.

"Gentlemen," the squad leader began, "this evening we will test your ability to properly wear the uniforms that the United States Military Academy has graciously provided to you."

The realization that we were not quite done for the day descended upon me.

"When I tell you to move, you will have five minutes to return to your rooms, put on your dress gray-over-white uniform, and return to me in this location for inspection. Are there any questions?"

There were none.

"Very well, then. Move!" he yelled.

When a young civilian first enters the U.S. Military Academy at West Point, the clock starts on an intense forty-seven-month experience. The first year is all about learning how to follow. Then, gradually, over the next three years, leadership opportunities are introduced. The goal of the Academy is to use each of these forty-seven months to blend academics, physical training, military skills, leadership experiences, and constant reinforcement of West Point's ethos—"Duty, Honor, Country"—to produce a well-rounded entry-level military leader with the potential to become much more.

One memory shared by every West Point graduate is the "clothing formation." It is a rite of passage for freshman cadets—called "new cadets"—during their first summer at the Academy. Cadets have six uniforms, some more formal than others, which they have to maintain and learn how to wear with great precision, including how a shirt, a collar, a belt buckle, or a pair of shoes must be prepared and worn. Learning how to wear them also means learning how to work together as a team.

"Welcome back, gentlemen," the senior cadet bellowed. He separated nine new cadets who had returned on time from three who had returned late. Fortunately (I thought), I was among those who had returned on time. He turned first to the other three.

"You three new cadets were late. There is no excuse for that, so I won't ask you for one. As a result of your inability to follow the simplest of instructions, the squad has failed."

Then he turned to the nine of us who had returned on time.

"You nine new cadets were on time." *We're about to be complimented, for a change,* I thought to myself. "However," he said, pointing to the three late cadets, "in your enthusiasm to take care of yourselves, you let your three classmates down. There is no worse failure than that."

At this point in the clothing formation, the squad is given a second chance, this time to go up and come back down in a different uniform. Usually, on the second try, they all return on time, but few of them are wearing the uniform properly.

"Good to see you all made it back on time, gentlemen. Perhaps you can be trained after all," the senior cadet loudly proclaimed.

This time we had agreed to meet in the latrine before heading back downstairs, to make sure we didn't leave anyone behind. It had worked.

"Now let's take a look at your uniforms," he said.

That didn't go so well.

"Gentlemen," he shouted, "two of you have returned wearing your uniform properly. The way the other ten of you are wearing your uniforms is an embarrassment to this military academy."

I was among those embarrassing the academy.

"But I am confused," he continued. "Since two of you obviously know how to wear the uniform, how is it possible that that knowledge has not been transferred to all twelve of you? You two new cadets who know how to wear the uniform have failed your classmates."

On the third attempt, the mental anguish of potential failure begins to give way to the physical anguish of running up four flights of stairs, frantically changing clothes, then running back down in the July heat. The third attempt is usually a bigger failure than either of the first two.

A fourth attempt yields no better results, and the exercise ends for the day with a lot of grousing by the new cadets—safely in their rooms, out of earshot of the seniors—that this is simply an impossible task.

A few days later, the clothing formation is repeated. At this point something interesting begins to happen. The new cadets begin to meet the standard in some but not all of the tasks. Twelve pairs of shoes pass the test. Twelve belt buckles are properly shined and aligned. Twelve collars are affixed to standard. But in the end, success in the entire task for all twelve cadets continues to elude them. The senior cadets acknowledge the progress but remain unforgiving of the new cadets for being incapable of following the simplest of orders.

The new cadets know they will soon face the clothing-formation challenge again. The senior cadets give them little bits of advice here and there, but mostly on their own they begin to understand that the clothing formation is less an individual than a collective challenge. None of them individually can meet the standard without the help of their squadmates. Roommates develop techniques to assist each other, to speed the process, and to give each other one final check before heading back downstairs for the inspection.

I'm not sure my squad ever successfully passed a clothing-formation inspection. But we did become a much more coherent group as a result of the experience. We felt a sense of accomplishment in coming closer to the standard each time. We learned that to succeed in this menial task, we had to work together, depend on each other, trust each other.

If the clothing formation were just an individual test, a few would have the individual talent and savvy to pass it. But because it was a collective test, it produced a sense of individual responsibility within the context of collective belonging. We all felt better knowing that when things went badly, we would *be there* for one another.

In any organization, leaders need to provide opportunities for individuals to see themselves in the context of group challenges, and individuals need to be reliable followers and take ownership of their own actions in the context of the group. One without the other isn't enough. Both are necessary to develop a sense of belonging.

THE BEST KIND OF MENTOR
FORT CARSON, COLORADO, 1979

In my early days I was a cavalryman through and through. I liked the mission, the spirit, even the swagger. After my tour with the 2nd Cavalry in Europe, I was posted to the 10th Cavalry at Fort Carson, Colorado.

The 10th Cavalry had a rich history in our Army. Nicknamed the Buffalo Soldiers, it had historically been a black regiment and had been assigned the unenviable task of taming the West during the Indian wars of the early nineteenth century.

In the late 1970s its mission was to be the "eyes and ears" of the 4th Infantry Division. This was an interesting time in our Army. We were still struggling to figure out how to transition from the draft Army of the Vietnam era to the all-volunteer force we hoped to become. It wasn't easy.

Our equipment was old. We were inadequately funded. Our personnel were weary of doing more with less. Fortunately, I soon realized, I was working for a leader who could turn all of our liabilities into opportunities.

Lieutenant Colonel Jim McWain was a 1961 graduate of Norwich University. He had served with distinction in Vietnam. By the time I joined him in the 10th Cavalry, he had been in command for about a year, so he knew the challenges and was well on his way to solving them.

Among the difficulties he faced—like most of his peers at the time—was an abysmal maintenance record. Report after report and inspection after inspection revealed that we just couldn't keep our equipment mission-ready.

When I arrived at Fort Carson, LTC McWain told me I was going to be his squadron maintenance officer. My heart sank. I had just graduated from the Captains Career Course and believed I was more than ready to be a cavalry troop commander—one of three in the squadron, each in command of fifteen combat vehicles and 120 soldiers with the mission of maneuvering in front of the division to find and disrupt the enemy.

Being told that I was going to be a staff officer for the next twelve to eighteen months was a terrible disappointment, and I thought I was being "farmed out" in favor of other captains in the squadron. LTC

McWain eased that fear during my in-briefing, but then he added to my anxiety in other ways.

LTC McWain's challenge to me was to design a comprehensive program at the squadron level that would train operators and supervisors and add an element of competition to the often-tedious business of maintenance. I knew it would be a daunting task.

It might actually have been too daunting, except that I had a world-class maintenance warrant officer working for me by the name of Bob Leslie. Bob was about my age and had just joined the squadron from Korea. When I told him of the challenge we had just been given, he enthusiastically set about developing a program.

When we "war gamed" it, we realized we actually had three challenges: we had to keep the fleet of tanks, armored personnel carriers, trucks, and jeeps running to meet our daily requirements; keep performing the quarterly and semiannual checks and services required by regulation for the equipment; and still find the time and resources to integrate the new maintenance training program into our daily activities. It didn't help that we were undermanned in some of the specialties we would require.

Given the authority and support to do so, Bob figured it out. He reached out to the division inspector general (IG) to briefly "borrow" a few experts to train the squadron's noncommissioned officers and officers how to inspect each type of vehicle. Then he produced a matrix— in the days before Excel spreadsheets—for a small group of experts he had personally trained to inspect each vehicle over the next three months with its operator and crew present. Finally, he scheduled each vehicle to return for a reinspection during which he and his experts would determine whether all faults had been corrected and all crew trained. A large billboard in the motor pool tracked the success of leaders in getting their vehicles through his program.

It paid off. Soon our maintenance rates were up, and we were one of the very few organizations in the division to pass the annual IG inspection.

Which gained the attention of the division commander.

One day, the two-star general in command of the 4th Infantry Division made an unannounced visit to our motor pool. He startled me as he walked into my office. Bob Leslie and I stood to salute him. This particular division commander was, as we politely described him, "old school." Very formal. Very conscious of protocol.

"Good morning, Captain. Where's your squadron commander?" he asked.

"Sir, I believe LTC McWain is in his office across the street," I replied.

"Well, get him over here. I'd like to talk to him."

"Yes, sir." With a gesture, I sent someone scurrying to find LTC McWain. "In the meantime, is there anything I can help you with, sir?"

"No, Captain. I have some questions I want to ask about the squadron's maintenance program, but I'll wait for the colonel."

"Roger, sir. Chief Warrant Officer Leslie here actually designed the program, if you want to discuss it with him while you wait," I offered.

"No. I'll just wait for the colonel."

The next five minutes were awkward. At some point, the general asked me where I was from and whether I was enjoying my tour of duty in his division, but mostly I recall uncomfortable silence.

Mercifully, LTC McWain arrived pretty quickly.

"Good morning, General," he said.

"Good morning, Colonel," the general replied.

"What can I do for you, sir?"

"Well, I have some questions about your maintenance program. You've had some real success, and I'd like to know what you're doing so I can see about replicating it across the division. Please walk me through how you got here."

"I could, sir," LTC McWain began, "but the two men you really need to hear from are standing right in front of you. Chief Leslie and Captain Dempsey put this program together, and I'd like you to hear from them. I'd be happy to add some context later on about how we fit this into the other things the squadron is doing." Then, turning to Leslie, he concluded, "Chief, why don't you begin?"

The general scowled. It seemed to me a menacing scowl. Then he turned, reluctantly, to Chief Leslie and me.

The briefing was actually uneventful. When it concluded, LTC McWain offered to escort the general back to our motor pool gate and to his waiting sedan. I can't say that we were sorry to see the general leave.

As they walked away, I wondered why LTC McWain had handled this interaction as he did. In those days, it wasn't often that a lieutenant colonel had the chance to impress a division commander—the senior officer who would determine his fate in future promotion boards. Maybe two or three times a year if he was lucky. All the colonels I had seen up to this point would have jumped at the opportunity to impress the boss. Moreover, it would have been normal for the most senior person present in any situation—in this case, LTC McWain—to seize the moment and dominate the conversation. Especially because this particular boss clearly preferred to speak to a colonel, not a captain. Yet LTC McWain had deferred to us, almost insisting that the general listen to us, and I knew it wasn't for lack of knowledge. LTC McWain knew everything there was to know about our maintenance program.

Something else, then.

About two days later I saw him walking around the motor pool and decided to ask him.

"Hey, sir," I said as I caught up to him. "Mind if I ask you a question about that visit by the division commander a couple of days ago?"

"Sure. What's your question?"

"Well, sir, he clearly wanted to talk to you, but you clearly wanted Chief Leslie and me to do the talking. I've heard you discuss our maintenance program, and you do it probably better than anyone other than Bob Leslie. So if you don't mind me asking, sir, why did you put yourself at risk with the division commander? It was almost like you were intentionally antagonizing him."

"You answered your own question, Marty. The best briefers on our maintenance program were right there in the room with us. You and Bob Leslie did all the work on this program and deserve all the credit." He paused. "Was that your first time briefing a two-star general?"

"Yes, sir, it was."

"Did you learn anything?"

"Yes, sir. Some things good and some not so good. If I had it to do over, I'd change some parts to make sure that what's really important stood out better."

"Good. Then the general's visit was a useful one. And by the way, I didn't antagonize the general. I just nudged him out of his comfort zone a bit." He smiled. "I'll see you tomorrow, Marty. You're doing a great job as our maintenance officer." With that, he walked away.

So that's what selflessness looks like in a leader, I thought. Always teaching, coaching, and encouraging. Giving credit, taking blame. I'd have done pretty much anything for LTC McWain in those days.

I would try to emulate him and create those moments for others in my own career. In any moment of success, I would always react by first asking ***who deserves the credit?*** There is simply nothing like believing your contributions matter to create a genuine sense of belonging.

IN THE MOMENT
BAGHDAD, 2003

In 2003 I was sent to Baghdad to take command of the 32,000 men and women of the 1st Armored Division. It was a time of great chaos more than a time of great danger, but that would change.

Beginning in the late summer of 2003, a capable insurgency began to assert itself on the streets of Baghdad. The remnants of Saddam Hussein's army had reorganized into a Sunni insurgency aimed at restoring the Baath Party to what it considered its rightful position in Iraqi politics. Not to be outdone, the Shia had formed a militia to ensure that they retained what they considered their rightful place in control of Iraq. We were caught in the middle, blamed and attacked by both sides.

My 32,000 soldiers were spread across Baghdad among approximately fifty relatively small forward operating bases (FOBs). Each day, hundreds of teams of four or five HUMMWVs carrying fifteen to twenty soldiers each would venture out of the base camps to go on targeted raids for high-value enemy individuals, to search neighborhoods, to assist in the delivery of essential services to the Iraqi people, to protect critical infrastructure, or to visit key political and tribal leaders.

We began to take casualties, initially from ambushes in the city's narrow streets and back alleys and later from massive roadside bombs placed along the highways.

Commanders at every level are trained to look for patterns. These can be patterns in the location of attacks, in the kind of attacks, or in the sophistication of attacks. They can also be patterns related to the movement and disposition of our own forces. With the help of my staff, I began to see that we were more likely to be attacked soon after exiting the safety of our base camps or just before returning. We were more likely to be attacked when we formed habits of movement, stopped routinely in certain locations—in other words, we were more vulnerable when we became predictable.

It was urgent that we communicate down the chain of command the risk of anything habitual and predictable in our movements and actions. Commanders at all levels emphasized this risk in patrol briefings and after-action reviews. For my part, I wanted to understand how well-trained and highly disciplined soldiers could fall victim to predictability, so I began a series of visits to FOBs to talk to soldiers before they ventured out on patrol.

Base camps are beehives of activity. Someone is always coming and going. Sentries guard the gates and carefully inspect vehicles before they are allowed entry. Small groups are always patrolling the perimeter of the camp, and a quick reaction force (QRF) is centrally positioned to respond to any unexpected attack. Soldiers not imminently scheduled to go out on patrol perform maintenance on their vehicles or weapons. Mess halls operate almost constantly, to account for the fact that soldiers are pulling sixteen- to eighteen-hour shifts. At some relatively safe location, groups will be conducting physical fitness training. About a quarter of the soldiers will be in their rest cycle, sleeping, catching up on hygiene, or staying in touch with loved ones at home.

Near the front gate, there is always a designated area where outgoing patrols stop and are told by the patrol leader to "lock and load" their weapons. Generally, within the base no one except sentries is allowed to have a loaded weapon, in order to limit the risk of an accidental discharge. So before going out the gate, patrols stop in this designated area to do their final precombat checks, load their weapons, and test-fire them into fifty-five-gallon drums of sand. It was in this area that I positioned myself to talk with the outbound patrol leaders.

As the lead of four vehicles stopped in front of me, I approached the patrol leader.

"How are you doing, Sergeant?"

"Good, sir."

"Where are you headed this afternoon?" I asked.

"Going to the Green Zone, sir. We've been instructed to escort someone from the embassy to a meeting with tribal leaders across the river."

"Okay. How many soldiers do you have with you?"

"Sixteen, sir."

"Are you here?" I asked.

"What do you mean, sir?"

"Are you here?" I repeated.

"With all due respect, sir, I don't understand."

With all due respect is soldier code for *What the f*** are you talking about?*, so I knew I had his attention.

"What were you doing before you mounted up for this patrol?"

"Well, sir, I was checking up on my soldiers and preparing myself."

"Anything else?"

"I was talking with my wife."

"How's she doing?"

"Pretty good, sir. Thanks for asking. I mean, she's got a few problems with the car and the kids, but she's working through it."

"Is she getting the help she needs?"

"For the most part, sir. But sometimes she's too stubborn to ask for help. It can be a little frustrating."

"I understand, Sergeant. Happens to all of us. I feel pretty guilty about it sometimes, actually."

"Yes, sir."

I put my hand on his shoulder. "Are you *here?*" I asked.

This time he understood my question.

"Got it, sir. I need to make sure I stay focused. I'm here."

"That's right. As you know better than anyone, you're in danger from the time you roll out that gate until the time you return. If you're not *here*, you put your entire convoy at risk. And you need to make sure everyone in this convoy is as focused as you are."

"Roger, sir."

We all have distractions in our lives. Some of them—like this soldier's family—are not distractions at all but part of the complex fabric of life. Others—like the vibrating iPhone or the omnipresent twenty-four-hour news cycle or the self-imposed isolation of earbuds— can indeed become distractions when we should be paying attention, accomplishing some task, or even just thinking. In any case, there are times when we have to compartmentalize the other things in our lives if we are to be effective leaders, trustworthy teammates, credible advisers, and reliable followers. It's a shared responsibility for each of us to **be here** when the team needs us to be here.

IN THE SITUATION ROOM
WEST WING, 2011

I became the eighteenth Chairman of the Joint Chiefs of Staff in 2011. My appointment followed the customary procedure: Each of the armed services nominates a candidate, who is required to have served as either a service chief or a combatant commander. The secretary of defense interviews and sends his recommendation to the president. The president interviews and makes his choice. Finally, the nominee appears before the Senate Armed Services Committee for confirmation.

Once I was confirmed, a transition team was assembled for me. It was composed of a senior two-star general, representatives from each of the services, and several prominent civilians with national security expertise. Their task was to study existing issues and assist me in developing a vision for my four years as chairman. In addition, the team looked ahead and prepared a six-month calendar for my consideration. They had two months to accomplish the task, and then we gathered for a day of briefings.

On the designated day, I walked into a large conference room in the Pentagon that had been prepared for the briefings. Arrayed on the table were four three-inch-thick binders, each covering a different aspect of the role of the Chairman of the Joint Chiefs of Staff:

1. *National security issues.* Here I would find a discussion of threats and opportunities around the globe, risk assessments from each of our ten combatant commanders, and a discussion of the state of our alliances and partnerships.

2. *The state of the armed forces.* This particularly imposing volume was a presentation of the size, location, readiness, modernization, and morale of our forces, the 2.1 million men and women of the Army, Navy, Air Force, Marine Corps, National Guard, and Reserve.

3. *Title X issues.* This was information on the mundane business of running the armed forces, including budgeting, recruiting, readiness, basing, demographics, discipline, and succession planning.

4. *National security processes.* This volume would tell me how I would spend the majority of my time over the next four years, including meetings with the service chiefs, the National Security Council, congressional committees (to whom I would also give testimony), and officials within the Department of Defense.

Over the next six hours, we drilled down into the transition team's work. The final two hours of the day were to be spent on the six-month calendar.

With great precision the team talked me through the period of October 2011 through March 2012. With enthusiasm they explained the order in which I would travel to meet our six U.S. combatant commanders—first, of course, the commanders in Iraq and Afghanistan, then those in Europe, Africa, the Pacific, the Middle East, and South America. Eagerly they laid out the order in which I would attend scheduled international conferences, including ministerials in Australia, NATO Chiefs of Defence (CHOD) meetings in Brussels, and a U.S.–Republic of Korea ministerial in Seoul. Confidently they described how I would visit other key U.S. allies and partners around the globe, including Israel, England, France, Germany, Japan, Egypt, Saudi Arabia, Jordan, Qatar, the United Arab Emirates, Turkey, and Pakistan. And they added that they were still working to arrange meetings with my Russian and Chinese counterparts.

When they were done, I leaned back, somewhat mentally exhausted at the prospect of so much overseas travel. And there was something else.

I turned to the head of the team. "Really comprehensive presentation, Colonel. Nice work. I'd like to ask you a few questions about your recommendations."

"Thank you, sir. Fire away," he replied.

"The trips to the two combat zones make perfect sense, as do the previously scheduled ministerials in Australia, Brussels, and Korea, but the rest of these visits are really at my discretion, correct?"

"Yes, sir, but your Joint Staff directors and the desk officers who manage the portfolios of the other countries were pretty adamant that you needed to get to these countries and meet your counterparts as soon as possible. And they were insistent that there's a particular order in which you should visit them, to ensure that you don't send the wrong message that some are more important than others."

"I understand," I said, "but why so adamant? Are we having trouble with some of them?"

"A few, sir, but we're in a pretty good place with most of them."

"Then why the urgency, Colonel?"

"Relationships, sir. Effective national security policy with our overseas allies and partners is all about relationships. Your staff—those working the portfolios every day—really want you to build strong relationships as soon as humanly possible."

I paused for a moment.

"Okay. I accept the premise that it's all about relationships. But take a look at the calendar you've just laid out."

The calendar was printed so that each month appeared on a sheet of paper approximately three feet long and two feet high. Laid end to end, they took up almost the entire length of the very long conference table.

"I haven't done the math," I continued, "but if I consider how many days there are in the next six months, it appears that I'll be traveling for most of them. At least two thirds by my estimation."

"Yes, sir, it does. If you'd like, I can list the countries in the order I was given them and draw a line separating the ones your staff most strongly recommends from the others."

"That may be the answer, Colonel, but stick with me for a moment. The recommendation you've presented to me is that I need to travel abroad to build relationships."

"That's right, sir."

"Well, is there anyone else I need to build a relationship with?"

"This is a pretty comprehensive list, sir."

"Well, how about here at home? What will be my most important relationships here in DC?"

"I'd imagine that it would be the SECDEF"—military shorthand for the secretary of defense—"the national security adviser, and the president. Probably a few others."

"I agree," I replied. "So where does this calendar make it a priority for me to build a relationship with the president?"

"It doesn't, sir. It looks like it assumes you already have a relationship with him."

"Right. But I don't. So what would you do if you were me?"

"I probably wouldn't travel much outside of Washington, DC, initially, sir."

"Good recommendation, Colonel! What I want you to do is take off any travel that I control. I'll go to Iraq and Afghanistan twice in the first six months. I'll go to the ministerials. And that's it. Other than that, I'll spend my time going to the SECDEF's meetings, to the National Security Council meetings, and to a meeting each week with the president. Then, once I actually have a relationship with the president, once I've built a little trust inside both the Pentagon and the White House, I'll begin to travel. So please go ahead and make those changes, and then I'll approve the calendar."

It turned out to be the right call. From the day I became chairman, I focused on building relationships in Washington, DC. I attended nearly every meeting I was invited to. I went with the secretary of defense each Tuesday afternoon to the Oval Office to meet with the president. I was a habitual presence at principals' meetings convened and chaired by the national security adviser. I spent time on Capitol Hill and visited the intelligence agencies and the State Department. I listened and learned the perspectives of senior leaders outside the Department of Defense, and I had the opportunity to share my perspectives with them. When I finally did begin to travel, I could teleconference or videoconference into meetings without any loss of effectiveness. I had taken the time to learn what it means to be an adviser to the most senior leaders of our government. I had learned to follow at the highest level.

But that learning wasn't over.

Six months later, I was notified of an upcoming meeting of the National Security Council on the Keystone pipeline. That morning I had been at Walter Reed Army Hospital for my one-year check-up after cancer treatment. I'd had a PET scan, a procedure that included an injection of a radioactive isotope. It was a nerve-wracking and tiring experience, but thankfully all was well. After my consultation with the doctor, I headed back to the Pentagon.

It had been a very busy week, and I wasn't real excited about going to this meeting. Uncharacteristically, I actually asked Secretary Panetta if I might skip it. He smiled and shook his head. We were a team by then, and I wasn't surprised by his answer. There were a few peripheral national security implications on this topic, but not many. I knew the meeting was going to be mostly about trade, commerce, energy security, and protecting the environment. I had only skimmed the briefing materials and had declined the pre-briefing that my staff had prepared for me.

After the usual harrowing ride in the secretary's convoy with lights flashing and sirens blaring through the crowded streets of Washington, DC, we arrived at the West Wing.

I can't imagine that anyone would ever tire of entering the West Wing of the White House for a meeting in the Situation Room. The history is so overwhelming, the issues so serious, and the stakes so high that my adrenaline always kicked in as I walked under the green awning and into the West Wing to be greeted by the security officer standing guard there. I'd been Chairman of the Joint Chiefs of Staff for a little more than six months and traveled across the Potomac River from the Pentagon to the White House an average of twice a week. I always enjoyed seeing the men and women who manned the security outpost just inside the door.

"How are you today, sir?" the guard asked.

"Good, Mike. Thanks for asking. You?"

"All is well, sir."

He glanced down at a monitor behind the desk, then looked up at me with an odd expression on his face. I didn't think anything of it.

I was the first one to arrive, but pretty soon other members of the National Security Council filed in. There were always place cards arranged around the table, and I spotted mine. I was a little farther down the table than usual—away from the president—due to the nature of the topic.

I exchanged pleasantries with the group. We met often, so we knew each other pretty well. I could see by the place cards that the vice president would not be in attendance, and I knew the secretary of state was traveling, so her deputy was attending in her place. Otherwise, the members of the National Security Council were all present. Added to the group for this meeting were the secretary of energy, the secretary of commerce, and the U.S. trade representative. I settled into my seat and arranged my papers.

Out of the corner of my eye, I noticed a flurry of activity outside the Situation Room door. Simultaneously, it dawned on me that the president was running late. He was sometimes delayed, but we were almost always informed about when he would join us. Not this time.

About that time, the head of the Secret Service entered the room. A great guy. I had known him for several years. I saw that he was approaching me. Most everyone was engaged in conversation, so no one else was paying attention as he leaned down and whispered in my ear.

"General, have you had any kind of medical procedure today?" he asked.

"Matter of fact, I did. I had a PET scan this morning. How did you know?" I asked.

"Well, you just set off every alarm at the front door," he told me. "We've had the president in hold until we figured out what caused it."

I thought back to my PET scan that morning. The technician had asked if I had any flights scheduled in the next twenty-four hours, because it would take that long for the heavy-metal radioactive isotope to clear my system. He'd told me that if I was going to fly, he could give me a card to carry with me explaining the medical procedure, because I would set off alarms from several feet away. Since I had no travel plans, I'd declined the card and forgotten all about it.

Until now.

"I'm so sorry," I said sheepishly.

He smiled. "No worries. A little drill every once in a while keeps us confident that the system is working as intended." With that, he walked away.

My face was glowing red. I'm not sure whether it was from embarrassment or from the radioactive isotope.

Not long after, I glanced up to see Pete Souza enter the room. Pete was President Obama's very talented photographer, and his appearance was always a sure sign that the president's arrival was imminent. A minute later the president entered. We all stood.

"Good afternoon, everybody," he said as he sat down at the front of the room. He asked who would be the first to speak, and the secretary of commerce kicked off the briefing.

About an hour later, the formal briefings ended, and the president announced that he wanted to go around the room and see if anyone who had not yet spoken had anything to add to the discussion.

I estimated that I would be the fifth or sixth council member to be called on, so I began—probably for the first time that day—to become interested in the meeting.

When it was my turn to speak, I smiled at the president and told him, "Unless you want to blow up the Keystone pipeline, Mr. President, I don't have much to add." There were chuckles around the room, and even the president smiled, but then he leaned back, and I knew he was about to use this as a teaching opportunity.

"You know, Marty, I really want this group to challenge each other's thinking. And mine. I don't want anyone just to show up; I need each of you to show up with the expectation that you'll contribute, even when the topic is outside your particular area of expertise. You may hear something that doesn't quite make sense to you. That's important. Or you may be able to make a connection with something that actually is in your area of expertise, and that could be important too. I'd like someone to surprise me. Help me think about these complex issues in a way that I may not have thought about them before. You get the picture."

"I do, sir. You've always made that very clear, and I should have been better prepared. Got the message, sir."

"Good. Let's move along."

First the alarm and now this. *Never too late to learn,* I consoled myself.

The president was right, of course. The reason the National Security Council exists is to apply a variety of viewpoints and expertise to the most difficult and complex challenges facing our nation. If it's going to achieve that purpose, its members have to be prepared and show up ready to contribute. I was fortunate that this experience came early enough in my tenure that I could learn from it. I made a commitment to myself that I would never show up unprepared and would always try to answer the president's challenge to "surprise" him.

Though this meeting wasn't my finest moment as an adviser to the president, it was a good reminder of what it means to be an inclusive leader *and* what he or she should be able to expect of a reliable follower. ***Following can't be a spectator sport.*** Those who are called upon to lead should be able to count on us to be more than passive observers in the leader-follower relationship.

There's no question that groups are more coherent, more collaborative, and ultimately more productive when members of the group feel a genuine sense of belonging, understand that their contributions matter, and are prepared to make them.

There should also be no question that developing that sense of belonging is a shared responsibility between leaders and those who follow them. Leaders must establish the climate, create the environment, and in word and deed reinforce that everyone belongs. But followers must "be there" for their efforts to bear fruit. Followers must want to belong and be willing to learn how to do so. They owe their leaders—and themselves—that much.

Because most who become leaders begin at some entry level, I contend that the best leaders learn to follow first.

In subsequent chapters, I will present other important attributes that leaders and followers must share if they are to develop the right kind of trust relationship. But it must start with a commitment to ***being there*** as the foundation on which to work and build, and that isn't getting any easier.

CHAPTER TWO

NEVER FORGET THAT CHARACTER MATTERS

THE INDEPENDENT VARIABLE
WEST POINT, 1970

"If you stand for nothing, Burr, what will you fall for?" These lines were penned for the character of Alexander Hamilton in the 2015 play *Hamilton,* by the brilliant Lin-Manuel Miranda. They are a paraphrase of an actual Alexander Hamilton quotation from our nation's earliest days.

It was also in the earliest days of our nation, in 1802, that Thomas Jefferson signed into law a proclamation establishing the U.S. Military Academy at West Point. It was believed then, as it is today, that professional military officers had to understand, respect, and protect the relationship between our military and our society, not merely with passing interest but with genuine conviction.

When young men and women enroll at West Point, they commit both to serve in the military upon graduation and to live their professional and personal lives according to an ethos of service. It's impossible to walk through the Academy's imposing Gothic architecture without noticing the frequency with which three "hallowed" words are chiseled into the stone of the buildings and monuments: "Duty, Honor, Country." As General Douglas MacArthur put it, these three words "reverently dictate what you ought to be, what you can be, what you will be."

West Point graduates, and the graduates of our other service academies, are expected to "stand for something." As cadets, we learned that underpinning the words "Duty, Honor, Country" were values that we were expected to embrace and that would define us—including courage, commitment, integrity, selflessness, respect, and loyalty. We received an education intended to produce first an individual of character and eventually a leader of character.

The pursuit of character becomes almost a religion at West Point. The words of the Cadet Prayer, recited frequently and with conviction, encourage young men and women "never to be content with a half-truth when the whole truth can be won" and "to choose the harder right instead of the easier wrong."

The choice of the "harder right" over the "easier wrong" is key to an understanding of character. Character is built over time in the choices we make; it is an accumulation of habits. It exists mostly in the privacy of our individual consciousness, but others get a glimpse of it in our behavior under pressure. It is reinforced in the little things we encounter in life, so that it is prepared for the big things that will inevitably challenge us. It is a willingness, invisible to others, to allow our aspirational self to confront our actual self and to influence our behavior so that our actions match our words.

Character is the independent variable in defining the leader-follower relationship. With it, the relationship is strong; without it, the relationship is weak.

Character matters at West Point because it matters afterward, in peace and in war.

BORDER PATROL
SECOND U.S. CAVALRY, 1975

In 1975, much of the U.S. Army was stationed in Germany as a deterrent to Soviet aggression. It's hard to imagine today, but thirty years after World War II, it was not uncommon to see U.S. tanks, artillery pieces, and trucks and those of our NATO allies on the roads and rails of what was then West Germany. My first assignment, as a second lieutenant of cavalry, was to a small outpost called Christensen Barracks, about fifty kilometers from the East German border near Bayreuth, West Germany. Our mission was to patrol the border as a visible sign of U.S. presence and resolve, as well as to report the activities of the Warsaw Pact forces—mostly Soviet—on the other side of the border.

I flew into Frankfurt's Rhein-Main Airport in January 1975. Not sure how to get from there to my new duty station, I made my way to the USO center in the airport. A nice young lady greeted me at the desk.

"How can I help you, Lieutenant?" she asked.

"Thanks. I'm trying to figure out how to get to my new duty station. It's in Bayreuth."

I pronounced it "Bay-root," which sounds a lot like "Beirut," so the young lady looked a little puzzled.

"May I see your orders, Lieutenant?" she replied.

"Sure. Here they are. You see right there, it says Bayroot."

She smiled.

"Actually, Lieutenant, your orders take you to Bayreuth, which is pronounced 'By-roit.' Let me get someone on the phone so you can find out what they want you to do."

"Thanks very much, ma'am."

Great start, I thought. Not long afterward, I had my instructions.

As an aside, forty years later, in 2015, I was invited to give the keynote address at a USO gala in North Carolina. When I recounted this story, a lady in the rear of the ballroom stood up and yelled excitedly, "That was me!" So it was. We had a good laugh about the experience afterward.

As I settled into my new role as a cavalry platoon leader, there were frequent challenges to the ethos I had embraced at West Point. Keeping aging vehicles running and ready was always difficult, and a negative maintenance report back to our higher headquarters would create a stir. More than once, some mechanic or motor sergeant suggested that we engage in "creative reporting" to avoid notice. I can't claim that I didn't consider it from time to time, but the other inner voice was always stronger. There were also personnel, training, and discipline issues to be reported. I had chosen this unit as my first assignment because of the autonomy and responsibility it offered at such an early stage in my career. Now I was learning that with autonomy and responsibility come tests of character.

Several times a week, I would lead a patrol out to the border myself. Generally, we stayed a couple of kilometers from the actual border, marked in our sector only by small two-foot-tall border stones. However, there were several spots along our route that brought us right up to the border.

During one of these patrols, which were generally fifteen to twenty kilometers and three to four hours in duration, I lost a communications encryption device. There were a couple of things that everyone knew could be career-ending incidents, and this was one of them.

The device was a CEOI, communications electronic operating instructions. In the days before we could encrypt radios with software, we passed messages by encrypting them manually. A series of letters and numbers encoded on one end was received and decoded on the other, using the CEOI. These operating instructions were used by all U.S. military personnel across Europe and changed about every seventy-two hours. If a device was compromised or lost, it affected not just that one unit but every unit on the continent.

We were about halfway through the patrol, and it was time for me to report our position. Those entrusted with the CEOIs wore them on lanyards around our necks to secure them. When I reached for mine, it was gone.

"Turn the jeep around, Sergeant," I said nervously.

"What's wrong, sir?" he said.

"I've lost the CEOI," I said.

"Holy s--t, sir. You are in deep kimchi."

"I know. Let's retrace our steps and try to find it. I also need to find a phone booth as quickly as possible and report the loss."

"Yes, sir."

Fortunately, after only a few miles, we stopped at a place where I had dismounted about thirty minutes earlier. The CEOI was lying on the ground about ten feet from a border stone.

"Damn, sir. Good thing you found it."

"That's for sure," I said. "Okay, now we need to find a phone booth."

"What for, sir?"

"I've got to report the loss."

"But you found it, sir."

"I did. But it was out of my possession, and it may have been compromised."

"I doubt it, sir. And if you report it, they'll have your ass for sure."

I had become fond of my job, and by all feedback I was doing pretty well at it. The platoon was beginning to come together. I paused. "Let's find that phone booth, Sergeant."

I had a terrific troop commander at the time, Captain Jim Noles, a Vietnam veteran and the kind of leader young officers wanted to emulate. I reached him by phone and told him what had happened.

"Thanks, Marty," he said. "We'll have to report this to Regiment and let them decide what to do about it. There will likely be an investigation. But we'll get through that together. Finish your patrol and head back here. I'll know more by the time you get back."

My heart was pounding as I returned to the border camp and reported to Captain Noles.

"As I suspected, Regiment is going to send an investigating officer to interview you," he informed me. "You probably realize that this could result in a letter of reprimand in your official file, which would not be good, or it could result in a letter of concern, which would not be made a matter of record. You did the right thing, and it will be my recommendation that this not have a long-term effect on you."

"Thank you, sir."

The next two weeks were a blur. The investigating officer was a serious, professional, and dispassionate major. He made sure I knew that the loss of the CEOI was a serious lapse. He noted that I had done the right thing by rendering the report even after I had found the device. He said he would file the report the following week and I should hear something soon after that.

A week later, Captain Noles called me into his office.

"I've got the results of the investigation, Marty," he said without expression.

"Yes, sir."

"I've been instructed by the regimental commander to counsel you in writing to remind you of your responsibility to protect the encryption devices entrusted to your care. I've done so in this letter." He held up a sheet of paper. "I will retain it under my control, and assuming you have no further issues like this, it will be destroyed when I change command. Do you have any questions?"

"No, sir. Thank you."

"You're a good young officer, Marty. Things happen. What matters is how we react to them. You reacted properly. Now get back to work."

"Yes, sir."

I had reacted properly, though not without a moment's hesitation and more than a little trepidation at the possible consequences. But that's the point. It is absolutely natural to experience a strong personal survival instinct in matters of character. The important thing is that this survival instinct must confront an even stronger instinct to live the way we say we intend to live. In that regard, character might be best understood as confronting yourself. That confrontation is one of the few things in life that we completely control. And that confrontation, and how it turns out, really matters.

TANK GUNNERY
GRAFENWOEHR, 1991

I took command of the 4th Battalion, 67th Armor Regiment in July of 1991. The unit had just returned from Operation Desert Storm, so there was a great deal of personnel turbulence and the monstrous task of returning to proper levels of readiness equipment that had been subjected to the harshness of desert operations and a month at sea. But battalion command is the dream of every young officer, and I was excited at the opportunity.

The battalion had fifty-eight tanks and about 550 men. They were a spirited bunch. Two years earlier, I had been the battalion's executive officer—second in command—so I was familiar with many of the officers and noncommissioned officers (NCOs). I was also very familiar with the battalion's rich history. A tank battalion's core competency is tank gunnery, the ability to put steel on target, and this battalion's reputation in gunnery was among the highest in all of Europe.

We were stationed at Rey Barracks in Friedberg, Germany. Stationed with us were another tank battalion, an infantry battalion, an artillery battalion, and an engineer battalion. There was plenty of good-natured trash-talking and spirited competition in everything from military training activities to sports.

A tank battalion, then as now, shoots gunnery twice a year. Each tank is manned by four people: the tank commander, a gunner, a loader, and a driver. The standards are tough. Ten timed engagements, usually seven during the day and three at night, under a variety of conditions. Multiple targets at various ranges, some in defensive positions, some on the move, and one in a simulated chemical warfare environment. The tank crew is graded on whether it hits the targets, but also on whether it executes its crew drill properly, safely, and with precise fire commands (the verbal cues exchanged among the crew members). To ensure impartiality, tank crew examiners are from outside the unit.

The tank battalion commander is expected not only to get all of his fifty-eight tanks successfully through tank gunnery but also to qualify his own tank with his own crew. There's a good bit of pride at stake among the fifty-eight tank crews about who will shoot the highest score. I was confident to the point of brashness about my tank crew, particularly because I had inherited arguably the best crew in the battalion from my predecessor. A perfect score in qualification is 1,000; 700 is a passing score. In their last gunnery, with the previous battalion commander, this crew had shot 995.

In Germany, tank gunnery is executed at the Grafenwoehr Training Area in Bavaria. Just getting all the people and equipment there is a logistics and transportation effort in itself, but we had managed to get everyone and everything there safely. I was feeling good about our chances of setting a new standard for the battalion during this gunnery, and also my own crew's chances of nailing a perfect score.

It is the tradition that the battalion commander makes the first run on Table VIII—the qualification table—to lead the way for the rest of the battalion.

This was not my first tank gunnery. In my eighteen years to that point, I had qualified probably a dozen or more times. But this was my first time qualifying as a battalion commander. We were confident. We had trained hard.

We moved our tank to the starting point, loaded and test-fired our weapons, did a final fire-control computer check, entered the temperature and barometric data, and awaited instructions from the control tower to begin.

Thirty minutes later we returned to the tower after completing the seven engagements of the day run. We had not done well. In fact, we had scored only 425 points out of a possible 700, thanks to a combination of missed targets and botched communications inside the turret among the crew. My crew was in a state of stunned silence. So was I. We'd need a near-perfect night run of 275 points just to qualify. I also knew that a tank battalion commander who fails to qualify his tank must live with the ignominy for the next six months until he has a chance to redeem himself.

As I dismounted my tank with the crew to go to the debriefing tent, I spotted my command sergeant major approaching. He was straight out of central casting: leather-skinned, a heavy smoker, and brusque, a real curmudgeon. There was a rumor that his picture had appeared on boxes of Ivory Snow detergent back in his youth; now he looked more like the Marlboro Man. I had known him for about four years. He had been the battalion's command sergeant major for the past seven and was fiercely protective of its reputation. I expected he would console me and my crew on the poor performance and encourage us for the night run.

"Rough run, sir."

"That it was," I replied.

"My advice is that if you don't qualify tonight, sir, don't stop at the tower. Just keep on driving back to the motor pool. You'll be done."

With that, he turned on his heel and left. *Well, that was encouraging,* I thought. My crew and I walked to the debriefing tent in silence.

There were no surprises during the debriefing. It's simple enough: to qualify, you have to hit the targets. We hadn't. My gunner, Sergeant Hall, was distraught. He clearly felt most of the responsibility.

"Okay, fellas," I said, "let's head back to the tank and get ready for tonight. We can do this."

I made the walk back to the tank with Sergeant Hall. He was a fine young man, and smart. He was really upset, and I could tell he was overthinking the task ahead of us. But he was well trained, and I wanted him to trust his instincts.

"How are you feeling about tonight, Gunner?" I asked.

"I'm a little nervous, sir. I don't think I've ever missed that many targets on a single run before."

"I've got an idea about that," I said. "I think I'm trying too hard to put you precisely on the target and taking too much of your time. Tonight, as soon as you indicate that you see the target, I'm letting go of the TC [tank commander's] override. That will give you more time to get the crosshairs on the target and pull the trigger. We'll be much better off with the turret in your control than in mine. We both know what you can do."

"Okay, sir. Sounds good. I don't think you're taking too much time, but I'll sure appreciate the extra second or two."

"You got it."

The adjustment I was describing to him wouldn't really make much difference—it was nothing more than standard operating procedure—but I wanted to share the burden he was feeling. He needed to both hear and feel that I still had confidence in him.

When we got to the tank, a turret mechanic was just finishing up his post-operations check of the fire-control system.

"How are you doing, sir?" he said to me. "I heard about your day run. Going to be tough to pull it out tonight."

"It will," I replied, "but we've had perfect night runs in the past. We can do it again."

I'm still not sure whether I believed this or was just saying it for the benefit of my crew, who were listening to our conversation. The turret mechanic leaned in a little closer.

"You know, sir, these fire-control computers can be finicky. I couldn't find anything wrong, but I've never seen you guys shoot so poorly. I might be missing something, so I could declare a fault and replace the computer. By the rules, that would give you guys another chance at your day run."

Another chance sure would be welcome, I thought. For just a moment I considered seeing if we could declare some mechanical or electrical fault and give ourselves another chance at the seven day engagements. But only for a moment. We both knew—and my crew knew—that the tank had performed to standard, but we had not.

"Listen," I said gently but matter-of-factly, "your job is to certify that the systems are performing properly. You've done your job. Now it's time for me to do mine."

"Yes, sir," he replied. "Good luck tonight, sir."

"Thanks."

After he had departed, my crew walked over to me.

"I heard what the mechanic said, sir," one of them offered. "You're right that we can't blame the tank for today's performance, and it wouldn't be right for us to get another chance when others won't. Thanks for owning this with us."

"Thank you for sticking with this washed-up tank commander," I replied.

They laughed.

I huddled with my crew to review what we were facing that night. We would fire first again, just after dark. We had three engagements, and we had to score 275 points in order to make sure that we had a qualifying score over 700. We went over each engagement in detail, then again, and again.

"We're ready," I told my crew. "I don't want any of you worrying about me or taking on more than your fair share of the burden. We're a team, and we'll either succeed or fail as a team. Now, go get something to eat and stop thinking about all of this for a couple of hours."

That night we made our run, scored a perfect 300, and qualified our tank with 725 points out of a possible 1,000. When all was said and done, our score was near the bottom among the battalion's tank crews. But we had qualified, and I was prouder of this accomplishment than of our performance in the next three gunnery periods, when we scored well over 900 points each time.

I was also proud that together we had pursued the harder right. Each of us, leader and followers. We had learned a lot about each other that day, and I'm not talking about what we had learned about tank gunnery.

THE SPECIAL ADVISER TO THE CHAIRMAN
THE PENTAGON, 2012

The Chairman of the Joint Chiefs of Staff has a small personal staff. Together they are tasked with making sure he—or, someday soon, she—gets where he is supposed to be on time, in the right uniform, and well prepared. Not just for meetings, but for speeches, media interviews, and congressional testimony, anywhere the chairman will be representing the two million men and women in uniform and their families. This last responsibility—representing the interests of the hundreds of thousands of family members who stand beside their soldiers, sailors, airmen, and marines—is especially important when the nation is at war.

In order to help me meet that responsibility, I set out to find a midgrade officer, male or female, who would advise me on family matters as a special assistant. I wanted someone who had demonstrated exceptional performance in previous military assignments and had the potential to reach higher ranks. I wanted someone who would be a champion for military families now and into the future as they continued to progress in their career. I asked my wife, Deanie, to help me in the interview process.

Of a pool of eight candidates, we decided to interview four, one from each of the services. At the end of the interview process, I turned to Deanie and asked her how she felt about each candidate. She knew what I meant. Each of the candidates had impressive credentials. The selection would come down to who had convinced us that they were passionate about the task of connecting with military families and not just in pursuit of the prestige of having worked for the Chairman of the Joint Chiefs of Staff.

Deanie responded immediately: "Major Michelle Donahue is number one."

"Okay," I said, "how about number two?"

"This is an important job," she replied. "We need the best possible candidate, and Michelle is it."

She was right. And I'd been married to her long enough to know that she had great instincts about people.

Michelle's answer to one question in particular had impressed us both. When asked to describe how she approached a task, she responded without hesitation that she believed it is not only what we accomplish but how that matters in our profession. She wanted us to know that she would approach each task with an open mind and provide her best advice regardless of whether it was precisely consistent with the initial guidance she had been given. In other words, she would speak her mind and provide her best advice without hesitation.

I hired her, and it wasn't long before her commitment to the answer she had given during the interview was tested.

Being the Chairman of the Joint Chiefs often comes down to deciding how to resolve competing priorities. There are always competing priorities in collaborating with the service chiefs to distribute the defense budget among payroll, infrastructure, maintenance, training, overseas operations, modernization, and family readiness. There are always competing priorities in deciding with the service chiefs how to distribute the military's capabilities in ships, aircraft, and ground formations around the globe among the six geographic combatant commands. There are always competing priorities in allocating the scarcest resource—time—among attending meetings in Washington, going overseas to engage our allies' military leaders, visiting troops at home and abroad, and visiting families, especially those of deployed troops.

One day, Major Donahue asked to see me at a particularly difficult time of competing priorities. Congress had just imposed a budget mechanism called sequestration. It wouldn't have a direct effect on our ongoing overseas missions, but it would affect our ability to prepare our servicemen and servicewomen to deploy. Although the budget seemed generous in its bottom line, we were stretched in significant parts of the armed forces. I was worried.

My executive officer, an Army colonel, came into my office as I was preparing for what I knew would be a contentious meeting with the service chiefs about the budget.

"Sir, Major Donahue said she needs to see you."

"What about, and can it wait?" I replied. "As you can see, I'm busy right now."

"It's about a family support issue that she's been monitoring, and she said it's important that she explain it to you as soon as possible."

"Well, send her in, but make sure this doesn't become a long meeting. I've got work to do to be ready for the chiefs."

Shortly thereafter, Major Donahue appeared across my desk.

When I became chairman, I had asked the staff to find me a desk with some historical significance and a few portraits of military figures from the past to hang on the office walls. They had done well. They found a desk at the Army War College that had belonged to Douglas MacArthur when he was the commander of Army Pacific forces in the Philippines just before World War II. It was impressive—about the size of a small aircraft carrier—and the scene was watched over by a portrait of General George Marshall that I had requested.

Though not my intention, the office and its historical artifacts were a bit imposing and intimidating. But not to Major Donahue.

"Good afternoon, sir."

"Good afternoon, Michelle. What's on your mind?"

"Well, sir, you recall that during our last trip Mrs. Dempsey and I learned that there was a problem with the funding for day care for the families of deployed servicemen and women. You told a group of them that you would look into it, and then you asked me to research the issue. I've done the research, and there is an issue. The program is underfunded. It's not being administered equally across the services. I'm also worried that sequestration will have a negative effect on it."

I knew that if this young officer had identified a problem, it was undoubtedly a real one. I also knew that with units unable to train, aircraft unable to fly, and ships unable to be maintained because of the budget mess, it was going to be difficult to move this item anywhere near the top of our list of priorities.

"Listen, Michelle, I understand the problem. But this one is going to be buried by the other budget problems we're facing. I'm meeting with the service chiefs later this afternoon, and I'll do what I can to get them interested in it. Thanks for bringing it to my attention. I'll let you know how it goes."

I looked back down at the paper I'd been studying when she arrived, expecting that she would depart. But she stood fast.

After a few seconds, I raised my head. I was a little irritated; time was running out before I had to go face the service chiefs. I could see that she sensed it. Nevertheless, she wasn't going anywhere.

"Is there something else?" I asked.

"Sir, you told me that you needed a champion for family support. Right now, this is issue number one. If it doesn't get addressed in this cycle of budget decisions, it won't get addressed for at least another six months. I just want to make sure you have everything you need to make the case with the service chiefs."

What she really meant was that she wanted to make sure I was focused on the issue. My irritation faded to admiration. Here was a young major pressing the Chairman of the Joint Chiefs of Staff to pay attention to something that I had said was important but had become distracted from. She knew she was taking some risk with her persistence, but she was willing to do so.

"Okay, Michelle, I get the message. And I think I know enough about the issue to make the case with the service chiefs and the secretary of defense."

She nodded. "Anything else, sir?"

"Just one thing," I replied. "Thanks."

This story is not about the meeting that followed. The service chiefs and the secretary of defense were great teammates when it came to matters related to family support. They enthusiastically favored restoring the budget necessary to provide child care for the families of deployed servicemen and servicewomen. Rather, this story is about a young officer speaking truth to power, about persistence, and about doing the right thing even when no one is watching.

Character is revealed not in the comfortable moments and not in the convenient moments. Character is revealed in the uncomfortable and inconvenient moments, the moments of personal risk, when outcomes are uncertain.

Young Major Michelle Donahue went on to be promoted twice and to command twice. She continues to lead and command with character.

A MORAL COMPASS
THE PENTAGON, 2012

In writing about leadership, I've described some of the items I keep on my desk to remind me what's really important: a walnut box filled with pictures of my fallen soldiers and engraved "Make It Matter"; a four-inch-tall crystal angel holding a gold star, given to me by a young girl who lost her Marine father; a framed dollar bill I exchanged with Sergeant Major Bernie Henderson in 1974 as an expression of my commitment to earn the trust of the soldiers I would soon lead.

I also have a moral compass. Well, actually, I have an antique brass compass engraved with the words "Moral Compass." It was given to me eighteen months into my time as Chairman of the Joint Chiefs of Staff by one of my aides-de-camp.

In the military tradition, generals and admirals are assigned aides-de-camp. They are generally responsible for making sure that the general or admiral gets where he or she is supposed to be, on time and in the right uniform, but they often become sounding boards, confidants, and trusted advisers. I had six during my time as chairman. Each made me a better chairman.

From September 2011 through December 2012, Lieutenant Commander Mike Wisecup was my aide-de-camp. A Naval Academy graduate, Navy SEAL, and Olmsted Scholar, Mike was tall and athletic, poised, confident, and inquisitive. Like most aides, he was clearly one of the best among his peers.

Even as a young officer, Mike could command a room. The chairman's social schedule is nearly as packed as his daily meeting schedule, and when Mike accompanied me to social receptions, my Army blue uniform and four stars were no match for his choker white uniform and the trident insignia of a Navy SEAL. Sometimes, as people gathered around him, he would catch my eye, grin, and shrug.

As we parted company in 2012, Mike surprised and touched me with a gift. It was an antique brass compass engraved with "Moral Compass" in the center of the cover and eight attributes at evenly spaced points around its circumference. On the back he had centered the word "trust."

Mike explained that he had heard me speak often about the importance of leaders having a moral compass, a set of principles to define their "true north" and to guide them as they navigate through difficult and often ambiguous decisions. He said that the most enduring lesson he would take from our time together was the importance of trust in building and sustaining relationships, whether with the most junior sailor or the most senior elected official. He said that he had selected the eight attributes for the compass because, based on our time together, he considered them the building blocks of trust and the defining elements of character.

My "moral compass" has been with me ever since. I've sometimes mused that I might add or substitute an attribute or two for those currently engraved on it, but in the end I've always decided that I couldn't improve on my young sailor's advice about how to find the right path and stay on it.

So here are a few thoughts about each of the attributes engraved on my brass moral compass.

Trust: The real key to any positive relationship between leaders and followers, and therefore appropriately positioned at the center of the moral compass. Everything we do should contribute to developing trust. Everything we are should reinforce that we are worthy of that trust.

Justice: Speaks to our responsibility to respect the law and to promote fairness. The best of us demonstrate genuine concern that our actions be perceived as fair and equitable by those around us.

Courage: On the compass in recognition of the fact that we must be willing to do the right thing even at personal risk. That includes leading from the front in conditions of discomfort and danger—physical courage—and making ethical decisions consistent with the values of the organization—moral courage.

Patience: Reminds us to take time to listen and to value the input of others. Those who act precipitously and unpredictably or who value only their own counsel are unlikely to act for the benefit of all.

Honor: Encourages us to do the right thing for the right reason without expectation of personal recognition or reward. Counsels that our reputation is our most precious possession.

Tact: Calls on us to be courteous and respectful, both because we should be and because we are more influential when we are not threatening. Knowing and appreciating what others have affecting their lives makes it more likely that our input will find a receptive audience. Tact is a reflection of empathy with those both senior and junior to us.

Loyalty: Provides us with the confidence that we will be there for each other when we are vulnerable. Loyalty must work both ways, cannot be blind, and must be earned.

Charity: Ensures that we remain mindful that there are many others whose lives are more difficult than ours. Charity is living with compassion and empathy.

Truth: A foundation of truth is the currency of the relationship between leader and followers. The best of us have the greatest respect for the truth and a passion for discovering it. We should "never settle for a half truth when the whole can be won."

Whether we lead or follow, from time to time we must take stock of ourselves. We need to understand what defines us. We need to compare our behavior with our beliefs. We need to think about what qualities we hope others see in us. We need to confront our aspirational character with our actual character.

Not all of us have a moral compass on our desks, but we need to have one in our hearts. Without it, we won't live a life in which character matters.

In this era of ubiquitous information, complexity, and intense scrutiny, it is becoming routine to respond to reports of character flaws in business, athletics, and politics with an indifferent shrug and a "Yes, but . . . ." It's becoming easier to rationalize a lack of character by emphasizing accomplishments, as though this were a binary choice. It's becoming commonplace that reports of character flaws are greeted with skepticism.

In this environment, character matters even more. Building teams requires bringing together individuals with the right credentials, commitment, and character. A lack of any one of these will eventually mean trouble. Our teams—both leaders and followers—will and should be judged not only by *what* they accomplish but also by *how*.

Neither leading nor following will be effective if personal interactions and beliefs are considered mere differences in perception. Rather, both leading and following require conviction and character.

CHAPTER THREE

BE PASSIONATELY CURIOUS

EINSTEIN'S ADVICE TO LEADERS
WEST POINT, 1984

I was a good student at West Point—probably not as good as I could have been or should have been, but I performed well enough there and in the eight years afterward, serving with two cavalry squadrons, that I was selected for graduate school and a teaching assignment back at West Point. I chose to pursue a master's degree in English literature at Duke University.

Even in retrospect, I wouldn't suggest that at the time I was passionate about getting an advanced degree in English. I *was* passionate about going to graduate school in some discipline other than engineering, my undergraduate major, and I really wanted to go back to West Point to teach. The English department provided a path for me to accomplish those goals.

I took this path against the advice of several of my closest mentors. The Army had just established the National Training Center at Fort Irwin, California, and senior captains were in high demand to provide the cadre at this important training facility. Some of my mentors argued that I should remain "current" and "in the mainstream." My instinct—thankfully reinforced by several other mentors—was that

I would benefit from learning to think better and differently, so I headed to Duke.

I arrived on campus in the summer of 1982, unsure of what to wear and definitely unsure of what I had gotten myself into. But I knew that I was about to experience something way out of my comfort zone, and I enjoyed the feeling.

Like most graduate students, I took my studies far more seriously than I had as an undergraduate. I sometimes think of my undergraduate studies as a survival reality show, but I wanted to do well in graduate school and felt I had the proper attitude and life experience to do so.

My fellow graduate students in the English department were an interesting bunch. Initially we had very little in common. All had majored in English literature as undergraduates. Most were doctoral students, some had already been teaching, and many had published articles about English literature in scholarly journals. It was more than a little intimidating, but I was committed to outworking them.

Among my first classes was a course on the Romantic poets of the late eighteenth and early nineteenth centuries. It required a lengthy term paper, and I chose to write about the poet William Blake because I was fascinated by the way he illuminated his books of poetry with artwork. I was certain I could discover something significant in the combination of poetry and illumination. For two months I labored through Blake's poetry and pored over his illuminations until I had settled on a topic. A month later, I submitted my term paper, sure that I would be rewarded with an A and be encouraged to publish my writing in some scholarly journal.

When a few days later my paper was returned to me with a B-minus, I was stunned. I knew that a B-minus was nearly the lowest grade possible for a graduate student who meets the minimum requirements of a paper and turns it in on time. So I scheduled a meeting with my professor, Dr. Victor Strandberg.

Dr. Strandberg listened patiently as I described how I had selected my topic, done the required research, and organized and written the paper to support my thesis. I explained that I had never worked harder on a project and ended my appeal certain that he would reconsider how he had evaluated my work.

"Well, Mr. Dempsey," he began, "it's very clear that you have worked hard on this project."

I smiled, surmising that I had persuaded him to raise my grade, if only a little.

"But," he continued, "although reasonably well written and reasonably well researched, it is neither interesting nor persuasive."

That can't be possible, I thought. *Surely he's going to say something about the effort.* He did.

"And to your point about effort," Dr. Strandberg went on, "we expect the best effort of all of our students as a matter of respect for the great poets we are studying and for each other. Ultimately, your grade is a reflection of what you have added to our understanding of the poetry—what you have produced—not what you have tried to produce. Your paper reveals your interest but not your enthusiasm, not your passion for the subject. I hope this will be helpful to you in the future. As for this paper, your grade stands as I presented it to you."

I hadn't seen that coming.

But the sting wore off, and Dr. Strandberg's words turned out to be helpful to me, and not just in the remainder of my studies at Duke. That may have been the first time I had thought about the difference between being committed to a task and being passionate about understanding it and getting it right.

Eighteen months later, in June of 1984, with master's degree in hand, I arrived at West Point to become an assistant professor of English.

Each year, in a large auditorium, the department's leaders introduced themselves to the one thousand new cadets and the thirty captains and majors joining the English department faculty. I recall wondering who was more nervous, the freshman cadets or the freshman instructors.

Soon the head of the department, Colonel Jack Capps, walked to the center of the stage. A 1940 graduate of West Point who had earned his doctorate in English from the University of Pennsylvania, he looked and acted every bit the part of an English professor. The audience quickly quieted at his appearance.

"Ladies and gentlemen," he began, "I hold in my hands two books with which you will become very familiar this year. One is Webster's dictionary. The other is the complete works of Shakespeare."

This is going to be interesting, I thought. He had the cadets' attention, mostly out of abject fear that they were going to be responsible for two such imposing volumes.

"This one," he said, holding up the dictionary, "will give you the definition of the words you encounter this semester." He paused and looked around the room. Once he was sure that he still had everyone's attention, he continued. "This one"—now holding up the complete works of Shakespeare—"will help you learn what the words mean."

With that, he turned and walked off the stage.

That's it? I thought. Looking around, I could see that the cadets' reaction was same as mine. At that point, other senior faculty members began to cycle on and off the stage to provide the cadets the administrative details of their coursework.

Back in my office, I thought about what Colonel Capps had just said. *Can what we're about to do this semester really be distilled down to learning what words mean?* I wondered.

As the semester went on, I began to understand and appreciate what Colonel Capps had meant. Of course, there is more to a course in English literature than learning what words mean. There's good or not-so-good grammar, correct or incorrect spelling, adequate or inadequate research, persuasive or unpersuasive analysis. But, in the end, it may just be that the most important thing a student can take away from a literature course is a thirst for a deeper understanding of what the work of literature means, both when it was written and as it is read today. Unless we are curious about what lies beyond the words, we will never learn the most important lessons available to us.

It was no less than Albert Einstein who said of himself, "I have no special talent; I am only passionately curious." Getting beyond merely being committed to some task to being passionately curious about it makes for a much more productive work environment and a much more positive relationship between leaders and followers.

THE AGT1500 M1A1 MAIN BATTLE TANK ENGINE
FRIEDBERG, GERMANY, 1991

As I mentioned earlier, in June of 1991 I took command of the 4th Battalion, 67th Armor Regiment in Friedberg, Germany. The battalion had just returned from Operation Desert Storm, where it had performed brilliantly.

After six months in the desert environment of Saudi Arabia and Iraq, the soldiers were understandably tired, and the wear and tear on their equipment was obvious. After a month of well-deserved leave, the first order of business was going to be bringing both the men and their equipment back to the highest possible standard of readiness. As a tank battalion, we would give the highest priority to the fifty-eight tanks assigned to us.

The M1A1 main battle tank is a superb piece of machinery: seventy tons of armor envelope in which four crew members are capable of maneuvering at speeds up to fifty kilometers per hour over almost any terrain while firing 120-millimeter projectiles at stationary and moving targets well over two thousand meters away.

Because the tank is their "home" while deployed, and because they spend so much time training with it and maintaining it every day, tank crews become fond of their tank. They are fastidious about keeping it clean, brag about it to their fellow soldiers, and even name it.

As imposing as it appears, there are a few things that require a good bit of "tender loving care" when dealing with a tank. One of them is the proper operation and maintenance of its engine.

The tank is powered by a 1,500-horsepower gas turbine engine. To generate the power necessary to move seventy tons with such speed and agility, the tank consumes enormous amounts of fuel and ingests massive amounts of air.

The tank's reliance on fuel is well understood by anyone who has ever been around a tank. It holds 525 gallons in two fuel cells, and when both are full, the tank can travel about 275 miles. Running out of fuel is considered the most egregious sin a tank crew can commit, so crew members carefully—almost to the point of paranoia—watch their fuel gauges to know when they need to report and request refueling.

Air-ingestion issues are often less well understood. The tank has half a dozen air-filter canisters cleaning the air it takes in, three on each side of the rear deck. And a series of rubber seals positioned around the engine protect it from ingesting sand, dirt, and dust along with the air necessary for its operation. Leaks in the air-induction system are serious. In a sandy and dusty environment, even a minor leak in one of the main rubber seals can allow gallons of sand into the engine in just a few hours of operation, leading to certain engine failure.

The air filters must be "blown out" at frequent intervals to remove dust and sand particles, and crew members are generally diligent in accomplishing the task. They are often less vigilant for problems related to the tank's air-induction seals. At least they *were*.

After our thirty-day post-deployment leave (called "block leave" because the entire unit takes leave at the same time) and another thirty days of post-deployment maintenance, we began to train. As we did, we began to experience an excessive number of engine failures, far more than expected based on engine hours and operational tempo. In troubleshooting these failures, we discovered that many of them were air-induction issues.

I was perplexed and more than a little miffed. Our tank crews and junior leaders should have been able to see these problems and correct them before they became failures. Maintenance is hard enough without adding to the difficulty through operator neglect. I sought the advice of my battalion maintenance technician, Chief Warrant Officer Roger Behrens.

Behrens was a living legend in the 4th Battalion, 67th Armor Regiment. He was smart, athletic, and personable. Though a technician by title, he was superb leader. He was also a stern taskmaster; young officers and NCOs knew they had better accomplish the maintenance tasks he assigned them—or suffer the consequences of his sharp tongue, tireless work ethic, and long memory.

I walked into his office in the motor pool.

"Hey, Chief," I said. "These engine failures from air-induction problems are killing us. It's affecting our ability to train, and I'm starting to hear from my boss that he's not happy about all the money we're spending replacing engines. You got any ideas?"

"I'll tell you what I'd do, sir," he replied. "I'd fire a few tank commanders, and maybe the rest will get the message."

I'd known Roger Behrens a long time, and he was one of the most thoughtful, dedicated, and humble men I'd ever served with. I doubted that he actually thought this was the solution, but he was clearly frustrated at our current state of maintenance.

"It might come to that, Chief. But are we doing everything we can at our level to influence things at this point?"

"What do you mean, sir?"

"I don't know. I keep asking myself whether the problem is that the operators don't know or that they don't care."

"That's a good question, sir. I can tell you with confidence that we've gone over and over how to clean the air filters and how to properly start and cool down the engine."

"I know you have, Chief. But do you think they understand why that's so important? Maybe we've only given them half the information they need. Maybe they'd be a little more enthusiastic about maintenance if they understood how it all fits together."

"Tell you what, sir. I like the idea of pushing this a little further. You're the trainer, but let me put together a proposal for how we might give them more than a set of instructions to be followed."

A few days later, he asked me to come back and see him in the motor pool. He was standing next to a tank power plant (engine and transmission) that had been lifted from the tank and placed on the ground behind it.

"What do you see here, sir?" he asked.

"A power plant."

"Right. Now I'd like you to walk me around it and tell me about the components and what they do."

"No can do, Chief. I mean, I can identify the engine and the transmission, and maybe a few other components, but I'd be hard pressed to tell you exactly what they do."

"Well, step over here, then."

He guided me to the back of the tank, where we looked into the empty hull.

"Can you point out and describe the seals that must be intact in order for the air-induction system to function properly?"

"Maybe," I replied sheepishly. "Where are you going with this?"

"Well, here's my suggestion based on our conversation the other day."

He proceeded to describe a training program that would fill in the blanks of why certain maintenance tasks were especially important. The first thing he would do was train me. Then, whenever a tank power plant was pulled for periodic servicing, platoon leaders and platoon sergeants would be required to walk me around the power plant, describing the components of the system and explaining how each one functioned. He believed that the prospect of being "quizzed" on the power plant by the battalion commander would be enough to encourage young officers and NCOs to get to know their tank better and, ultimately, take better care of it.

"Interesting, Chief. Let's give it a try."

"Great, sir. I'll let the battalion's junior leaders know they will soon have a chance to impress you with their knowledge of the tank engine."

It took me a few hour-long sessions with Behrens over a couple of weeks before I was confident enough about the tank engine to begin working with the battalion's junior leaders. Then, once a week for about the next twenty weeks, I spent an hour with one or two junior leaders walking around the tank engine. Initially they were anxious about these sessions, but eventually they came to see them as an opportunity for us to get to know each other and to learn from each other.

And the program *worked*. Armed with the additional knowledge, junior leaders began to challenge their soldiers to know their tanks better. Steadily, maintenance rates improved. Even more important, young officers and NCO leaders began to understand that with leadership comes the responsibility to continue learning and to be perpetually curious about their responsibilities, not just work through a checklist of tasks each day. They began to express greater interest not only in the tank's air-induction system but also in its electrical and fire-control systems. They began to strive to become experts on the tank, not just crew members with a narrow scope of responsibility for its operation. Greater expertise in the "system of systems" that is a tank led to better performance.

Encouraging curiosity takes effort. It's unreasonable to expect it to occur on its own. Encouraging curiosity to become enthusiasm, perhaps even passion, requires an appreciation of why it's important and a shared commitment among leaders and followers.

THE CHAIRMAN'S CAMPAIGN OF LEARNING
THE PENTAGON, 2011

When I became Chairman of the Joint Chiefs of Staff in September 2011, I asked the Army's Center of Military History to loan me the official portrait of General George C. Marshall when he was Chief of Staff of the Army to hang in my office. They agreed, and soon it was hanging in my office, positioned where it appeared that the famous general was watching me as I went about performing my duties. When faced with an especially perplexing problem of national security—a frequent occurrence—I would often ask myself, *What would George Marshall do?*

Marshall was a particularly noteworthy, selfless, and inspirational leader. He was a voracious reader who considered himself a student of multiple disciplines, from history to economics to military operations to diplomacy. Both President Roosevelt and President Truman counted him among their most trusted and influential advisers. Between 1939 and 1951, Marshall served as Chief of Staff of the Army, special envoy to China, secretary of state, and secretary of defense. As secretary of state, he authored the plan to reconstruct Europe following World War II (the "Marshall Plan"), and in 1953 he was awarded the Nobel Peace Prize. Marshall's special talent lay in seeing connections that others often missed. It served him well in peace and in war.

I wanted to be able to see the connections in our time as Marshall had in his.

As I began my tour of duty as Chairman of the Joint Chiefs of Staff, I knew that my education and experiences over the previous thirty-seven years had served me well in a variety of roles and responsibilities, but I recognized that I would have to keep learning—and make learning a priority—if I was to be an effective adviser to the president and an effective teammate of the Joint Chiefs.

In the work I had done to prepare for the role, I had learned that my responsibilities generally fell into two broad categories:

1. Advising the president, the secretary of defense, and the National Security Council on emerging issues affecting the state of our relationships with our close allies and partners, including but not limited to threats posed by nation-states and terrorist networks,

cybersecurity, social media, robotics, artificial intelligence, pandemics, energy security, and migration.

2. Collaborating with the Joint Chiefs on emerging issues affecting the state of civil-military relations within our country, including the military's relationship with the executive branch, the legislative branch, other government agencies, the media, and, equally important, the American people.

Because in Washington the budget drives all, I knew I would also have to master the time lines and inputs of the federal budget process.

It was a daunting task list.

From my predecessor, Admiral Mike Mullen, I had inherited two superb young officers who served on the chairman's personal staff as a small "think tank." Jim Baker was an Air Force colonel and, it didn't take me long to figure out, quite simply one of the smartest men I've ever known. He was quiet and unassuming but remarkably well networked and highly trusted inside the Pentagon and in many other offices across Washington, DC. He knew how our government functions—a surprisingly uncommon trait among those who live and work in our nation's capital—and he had an uncanny ability to anticipate and understand challenges before they became crises. Sam Neill was a Coast Guard commander. Also very bright, articulate, and humble, his "superpower" was networking in Washington and with many of the best academic institutions in America to monitor the state of civilian-military relations.

Within just a few days of becoming chairman, I summoned them to my office and asked them what they would do to make learning a priority if they were in my position.

"Sir, your greatest challenge is your schedule, and your scarcest resource is time," Jim began. "Whatever you decide to do will have to account for the fact that eighty percent of your schedule is out of your control."

"That's right, sir," Sam put in. "Just making something a priority isn't going to do much good. Your life as chairman is really an exercise in managing competing priorities."

"Doesn't sound very promising, fellows," I said, stating the obvious.

"Well, sir," Sam said, "we had a heads-up that this is what you wanted to talk about, and we've actually been thinking about a few ways to help you."

"What do you have in mind?"

"We need to build a Campaign of Learning for you, sir," he continued. "We propose that you allow us to put something on your calendar once every couple of weeks that will give you an opportunity to learn about a topic outside of your obvious military expertise. Sometimes we'll ask you to travel for this experience, and other times we'll bring the experience to you here inside the Pentagon."

"What kind of opportunities do you have in mind?"

Jim took the lead. "Well, there are a few areas we can see right now where a better understanding will benefit you in your discussions with the other members of the National Security Council. For example, the spread of infectious diseases like Ebola in West Africa, the weakening of the euro overseas and the effect it could have on our military presence over there, the growing cybersecurity threat, and the impact of emerging technologies like 3-D printing, artificial intelligence, and robotics on national security. Others we may not be able to see right now, but we'll watch for those and propose to you that we include them in the Campaign of Learning."

"This is really interesting," I said, "but is it realistic? I mean, do you think we can really pull this off with everything else happening around us?"

Sam was ready for this one. "Sir, for this to work, you've got to make it clear to everyone that this learning is not something arbitrary or discretionary. You've got to make it clear that this is an important part of your responsibilities as chairman."

"And just how do I do that?"

Sam again: "We need four things from you, sir. First, we need you to direct that we get a seat at the table at the monthly calendar meetings with your executive officer. He runs a tight ship, and unless we're at the table, the rest of the staff is going to capture every available second of your time."

"Okay," I said.

"Second, we need you to agree to a realistic frequency for these events. We think not more often than every two weeks and not less than every month."

"Let's make it every three weeks until we see how it goes," I replied, "and I want you to do your best to blend these events into my other scheduled travel. It will be a lot easier to add a half day to a trip here and there than to plan a separate trip."

"Roger, sir. Third, we'll need you to approve the topics far enough in advance that we can make sure you get to meet with the right level of folks when we take you someplace."

"I can do that," I said.

"And fourth, we really need you to commit to attending these events, even when the rest of the staff will give you a dozen reasons why you can't afford the time as the event gets closer. When we get the right person to meet with you on these important topics, it will be embarrassing and damaging to our relationships with them if we cancel at the last minute."

"I understand," I assured them. "If I agree to it, I'll do it. I have great confidence in the vice chairman, and he can put out any fires that might come up in my absence. Anything else?"

"No, sir. We'll take it from here."

Jim Baker and Sam Neill were tenacious in making sure I remained curious and that my curiosity made me more relevant during my time as chairman. Over the next six months I met with Laurie Garrett, an expert on pandemic diseases and author of *The Coming Plague*. I was visited by Ben Bernanke, chairman of the Federal Reserve. I visited Mark Zuckerberg and Sheryl Sandberg at Facebook. I traveled to talk with cybersecurity expert Kevin Mandia and to tour the AT&T Network Operations Center in New Jersey. Each meeting opened my eyes to something new, and I could sense that these were issues that wouldn't remain new for long. They were about to become very real challenges for our country.

In addition to Laurie Garrett and Ben Bernanke, I had one other visitor to my office as part of my Campaign of Learning during those first six months.

Early one afternoon, I was returning from my morning meeting with the secretary of defense. His office was directly above mine in the E-ring of the Pentagon, a relatively short walk through the long, wide corridors. As I came down the stairs and turned the corner toward my office, I saw that a crowd of fifty or sixty military and civilian personnel had gathered in the hallway.

"What's going on in the hallway near my office?" I asked my aide-de-camp.

"Don't know, sir. Hold up a second and let me look at the schedule."

Fifty feet ahead of us, the crowd was still growing.

"Sir," my aide-de-camp informed me, "the schedule says you have a meeting in five minutes in your office with the special envoy to the United Nations High Commissioner for Refugees."

"Who's that?" I asked.

"Angelina Jolie, sir."

That explained the crowd.

Our meeting was interesting. Through her lifelong commitment to humanitarian work, Angelina Jolie has gained a real appreciation for the way global issues affect refugees and displaced persons. She reinforced and strengthened my belief that migration is a problem that can be solved only through collaboration between governments and nongovernmental organizations. She predicted, correctly, that this problem would continue to get worse until nations stopped thinking about it as a problem to be solved at their own borders. We met in the spring of 2012. The Syrian refugee crisis was then unfolding and, as it did, the security situation in southern Europe and North Africa became much worse.

As she left my office, she graciously greeted several dozen admirers.

One of the most memorable events in my Campaign of Learning was a visit to the Library of Congress. The ten combatant commanders had all been summoned to Washington, DC, for a meeting with the secretary of defense, and I asked them to arrive a day early and join me at the library. At our request, the librarian had arranged a display of artifacts illuminating how senior leaders in the past had made decisions in times of crisis. President Kennedy's items from the Cuban Missile Crisis were particularly fascinating.

In the middle of the crisis, while listening to a briefing from his close advisers, President Kennedy had been doodling on a notepad. On the notepad were a series of words, some circled and some crossed out, but also sketches of a mushroom cloud, a chessboard, and a sailboat. These sketches gave us real insight into the inner thoughts of the man who was about to make the most profound decision of his presidency. He knew the stakes of a potential nuclear conflict with the Soviet Union. He knew that he needed to make a series of thoughtful and carefully considered moves in order to outmaneuver his adversary.

And, in that moment, he felt the burden of leadership and clearly wished that he were somewhere else.

Ultimately, he made the right decision, despite some advice that could have taken us down a far more dangerous path. This display of Kennedy's artifacts reminded our group of military leaders that, in our interactions with senior civilian leaders, we should remember that there will always be an element of the human dimension to be considered.

Events in my Campaign of Learning were usually the most interesting part of my schedule. True to my promise to Jim and Sam, I made sure each event was faithfully executed. True to their commitment to me, they worked hard to find the kind of opportunities and to build the kind of relationships that would keep me curious and ultimately make me a better chairman.

Over the course of four years, I built relationships with the most influential thought leaders across the country. I found that the more I learned, the more I realized how much there really was to learn. I came to appreciate that national security is a patchwork quilt of anything that can be destabilizing to us or our allies. It isn't just about military threats.

I find it a challenge that, although we have access to almost anything we want to know in today's digital world, we often confine ourselves to that which reinforces what we want to believe. Perhaps it's all just too overwhelming; perhaps we fall victim to the comfort of confirmation bias; perhaps we convince ourselves we're just too busy.

Yet we can all contribute to the common good and to our common goals when we are better informed, when we can see connections, when we are a little more curious.

CHAPTER FOUR

UNDERSTAND THE LIMITS OF LOYALTY

THE CADET HONOR CODE
WEST POINT, 1970

In those early days at West Point, we learned that the team was *every-thing*. Individual performance mattered, but team performance was the ultimate measure of success. We were groomed to be battle buddies. We were expected to take care of each other, to have each other's back. Loyalty to the team was not an aspiration; it was an expectation.

Then they introduced us to the Cadet Honor Code, and we learned that loyalty actually has limits.

The honor code holds that "a cadet will not lie, cheat, steal, or tolerate those who do." There is no time off from the standard of honor, no excuses, no looking the other way. And West Point's honor code applies not just to academics but to every facet of cadet life.

The toleration clause is a particularly gut-wrenching part of the code, requiring absolute commitment, even if it means reporting violations by friends, classmates, and teammates. A former chairman of the Honor Committee summed it up this way: "There are two parts to being honorable: one, believing in it, and two, living up to it" (David Wilkie, class of 1988).

When a cadet is accused of violating the honor code, an investigation ensues, and any infraction is considered by a board of the cadet's peers. If the board determines that he or she has violated the honor code, the case is sent to the superintendent of the Academy with a recommendation to either dismiss the cadet from the Academy or suspend separation for rehabilitation.

On average, West Point conducts 120 investigations, which yield sufficient evidence to hold 65 honor boards, and ultimately finds 38 cadets in violation of the honor code each year. About a third of those found to have violated the honor code are dismissed, a third resign during the process, and a third receive suspended separation, essentially a second chance based on extenuating circumstances. Nurturing the concept of honor is serious business at West Point.

The premise behind the honor code is as old as the Academy itself, founded in 1802: an officer's word is his bond. The formalization of this unwritten code began in 1922 during General Douglas MacArthur's tenure as superintendent, when he formed the first Cadet Honor Committee to review allegations of honor infractions. In 1947 General Maxwell Taylor drafted the first official honor code. Though failure to report infractions was always considered grounds for expulsion, the code wasn't formally amended to expressly forbid toleration of others' infractions until 1970.

What makes West Point's honor code so challenging is that it is in tension with the idea of loyalty to the team.

As cadets we were taught to internalize the fierce team loyalty that is necessary for units to perform in combat—but also to recognize that loyalty has limits. These two ideas, each important, were intentionally held in tension, because it was only by holding them in tension that we could fully understand and appreciate each of them.

Loyalty is not an entitlement. It must be earned, both by leaders and by those who follow them. And even when loyalty has been earned, it must have limits. (Who among us can forget being asked by our chiding parents, "If your friend told you to jump off a bridge, would you do it?") Every day we see misplaced loyalty contributing to problems such as bullying, hazing, sexual harassment, discrimination, and corruption.

To be sure, it can be difficult to say no to someone in a position of power who is using loyalty as leverage, especially when that person makes it clear that they expect total and unconditional loyalty. But that's where loyalty must meet moral courage, if we are to act honorably and do what's right.

THE SURGE

BAGHDAD, 2007

Two senators and one congressman sat across from me in my headquarters in Baghdad in early 2007. I had been briefing them on the status of the Iraqi army, which I was charged with developing. Now they wanted to know if I supported the surge, a plan to significantly increase U.S. forces in Iraq that was being discussed extensively in Washington, DC.

"Well, sir," I began, addressing the senior senator, "I've been asked that question by both General Casey [the U.S. commander in Iraq] and General Abizaid [the commander of all U.S. forces in the Middle East]. I told them that I have concerns about what a significant increase in U.S. forces will do to development of the Iraqi army. We've made some progress putting them in the lead, but it's tenuous. If we roll in and take charge of places that we've turned over to the Iraqis, it will set them back."

"So you *don't* support the surge?" the senator snapped. I could see that he was agitated by my response.

"I didn't say that, sir. In fact, as you know, there are two of us three-stars here in Iraq, one responsible for combat operations and the other for building the Iraqi army, and we're still in the process of giving General Casey our advice. As far as I know, he hasn't made a decision. Once he does, we'll all support whatever decision he makes."

"Well, we're about to lose this war while you worry about building the Iraqi army, General. The president, several very senior active and retired military officers, and many of us on the Senate Armed Services Committee believe we need the surge, and we need it now. I question your judgment, and it sounds to me as though you're being disloyal in the advice you're giving."

"Absolutely not, sir."

"Well, we're done here, General." He stood and left the conference room.

I had never been called disloyal before. The accusation really stung at the time, and it would affect my relationships with several senators for years afterward. That's the end of the story; here's how I had found myself in this situation.

Thirteen months after I took the 1st Armored Division home to Germany from Baghdad in July 2004, I returned to Iraq to lead our efforts to build the country's security forces. It was a daunting but important task, generally considered the key to reducing the U.S. military presence in Iraq. As the thinking went, when they stood up, we could stand down.

My predecessor, General Dave Petraeus, had done a terrific job getting thousands of young Iraqi men to enlist and arming them for the very difficult battles against Al Qaeda and against several Shia militias in late 2004 and early 2005. When Secretary of Defense

Rumsfeld chose me to replace General Petraeus, he told me that my task was to turn the nascent Iraqi army from loosely organized groups of armed men totally dependent on the U.S. military into an independent institution supportive of and loyal to the government of Iraq and capable of assuming responsibility for their country's security.

The totality of their dependence on us was staggering. We recruited them, paid them, armed them, organized them, housed them, fed them, transported them, directed their combat operations, and provided medical care when they were injured or wounded. Making them independent would take time.

The first step was to convince the Iraqi government that the time had come for it to pay its own soldiers. Many—probably most—of these soldiers were not yet convinced that their government could be relied upon. We needed the Iraqi government to begin paying its soldiers, both as a practical matter and as an expression of loyalty to them. That meant we needed to develop both combat units and an institution to support them—an Iraqi ministry of defense.

The ministry had to become capable of budgeting and contracting, dispersing and accounting for funds, and procuring and distributing weapons and ammunition. In those early days, the Iraqi army numbered just over 100,000 soldiers, and the potential for corruption in matters of money—both at the ministry level and among senior commanders in the field—was extraordinarily high.

It took time, but we began to make progress. There were, of course, missteps along the way. For example, early on we discovered that the Iraqi civilian contractors selected by the Ministry of Defense to provide food, water, electricity, and waste removal to Iraqi units in Al Anbar Province were embezzling vast amounts of money, to the point where the individual soldiers were not receiving nearly what they needed to survive, let alone develop.

The scheme went like this. In the ministry's budget, each Iraqi soldier was allocated the equivalent of $12 a day for life-support services. So, for a battalion of five hundred soldiers, the ministry was expected to enter into a contract with a local private company to provide goods and services for $6,000 a day. However, one deputy minister had coerced a subcontractor to provide the services for $10 per soldier per day, allowing the deputy minister to pocket $2 per soldier per day. That subcontractor then found another subcontractor who pledged to provide the same services for $8 a day, and so on, until the individual Iraqi soldier was receiving less than half of what had been allocated for him. It was scandalous.

When we confronted the minister of defense with the results of our investigation, he did the right thing and corrected the situation. But in a country where tribes, political parties, and religious groups had not yet agreed to work together for some common good, we lived the reality that progress was usually measured by two steps forward and one step back.

We had similar challenges in training and equipping the combat battalions of this aspirational army. It was one thing to measure the number of personnel assigned, the amount of equipment provided, and progress in accomplishing a set of specified training tasks. It was quite another to measure the coherence of the battalions, the courage of the individual soldiers, and the integrity of their leaders.

In these early days, there was no functioning banking system in Iraq, so payroll was passed in cash from the Ministry of Defense to division commanders, then down to battalion leaders for dispersal to the soldiers. On more than one occasion, we discovered battalion commanders inflating the number of soldiers they claimed were assigned to them or covering for those who had deserted, in order to reap the extra cash for these "ghost soldiers."

Supply records were generally good, but it was not uncommon for me to receive reports that boots or uniforms or even rifles and ammunition were in short supply in certain battalions when I knew the items had been sent. As it turned out, old habits die hard, and some supply personnel who had served in Saddam's army would hoard equipment out of fear that senior leaders might hold them responsible if something was lost or destroyed. Others would extort money or benefits for providing equipment that should have simply been released to those who needed it.

Nevertheless, with time and patience and intense scrutiny, we started to see the outlines of an army that could begin to do more so that we could do less.

Each week we produced an assessment of the Iraqi army battalion by battalion, measuring all the capabilities necessary to succeed on the very complex battlefield that was Iraq. As battalions achieved the standard, we turned them over to Multinational Corps–Iraq (MNC-I), where they were paired with a U.S. battalion for joint combat operations. Once MNC-I assessed that they could operate independently, the U.S. battalion would turn over to them certain responsibilities, then eventually all. It was a painstaking process, but when Iraqi battalions achieved independent status, there was a noticeable improvement in their morale and performance.

As all of this was going on, the insurgency in Iraq was gaining strength. Most of it was caused by the Iraqi government's inability to show various groups that it would deal with them all fairly. Some was caused by the open border with Syria and an influx of foreign fighters, some was due to Iranian influence, and some was caused by seams and gaps in the transition of responsibilities from U.S. forces to the Iraqi army.

Back in Washington, anxiety grew as civilian casualties increased, as parts of Iraq—notably Al Anbar Province—fell under the influence of Al Qaeda in Iraq, and as Baghdad itself seemed poised to break out in open civil war between Sunni and Shia militias. While it had always been understood that progress would not be linear in such a complex environment, some were losing confidence in a campaign plan that relied on the Iraqis to take a greater share of the security load over time. One of my mentors had warned me when I took the job training the Iraqi army that "democracy is impatient and doesn't do long wars well." He was right.

By the fall of 2006, nearly everyone had concluded that we needed more U.S. forces in Iraq to confront the rising insurgency and better protect an Iraqi population that was beginning to lose hope. The question was how many additional U.S. forces to introduce and when to deploy them. General Casey sought the advice of his two three-stars, General Ray Odierno and me.

As the commander responsible for combat operations, Ray was understandably eager to get as many additional U.S. forces as possible and to get them as soon as possible. As the commander responsible for transitioning the fight from us to the Iraqis, I was understandably eager to make sure that whatever we did wouldn't dramatically set back the development of the Iraqi army. To me, that argued for a more limited and phased surge.

My advice, and the way in which it was conveyed, wasn't disloyal—in fact, just the opposite. In the face of significant momentum for a surge, it would have been easy to conclude that there was no sense rocking the boat against a tide already moving in that direction. However, to his credit, General Casey made it clear that he wanted our advice based on our judgment about what it would do to the particular missions we were tasked with. That's what we gave him.

Ultimately, the president decided to immediately send five additional brigade combat teams to Iraq. With the decision made, the discussion ended, and we all did whatever we could to make the mission successful.

The point of this story is not to debate the wisdom of the surge or its success but rather to examine how loyalty is measured in relationships between leaders and followers. Up to the point where decisions are made, it's important for leaders and followers to understand that disagreement isn't disloyalty. One of leaders' most important responsibilities is to establish an environment in which that distinction is clear to everyone. If they fail to do so, advice is unlikely to be forthcoming and even less likely to be honest.

It's also worth noting that loyalty is often transactional between leaders and followers when matters of judgment are at stake but must never be transactional when matters of legality and ethics are at stake. Stated a bit differently, there may be shades of gray in evaluating individual judgment, but not in evaluating individual behavior against existing standards of law and ethics. We should be loyal to each other, but that loyalty should have clear limits.

BUDGET BATTLES
THE PENTAGON, 2014

"The Tank" is a secure conference room in the Pentagon where the Joint Chiefs of Staff meet weekly, and sometimes more often, to grapple with the national security issues of the day. The conference room is named for a similar one at Fort McNair used by our predecessors during World War II. Windowless and austere, it had the feel of holding a meeting inside a water tank.

As the chiefs of each of the services met with me in the Tank in October of 2014 to discuss the projections for defense in the proposed federal budget, we knew we had a problem. By our estimates, if the budget was finalized in its current state, we would fall $25 billion to $30 billion short of what we needed to execute the national security strategy.

Time was not on our side. There's a saying in Washington: "The budget is real. Everything else is just rhetoric." It was true. The real priorities of government are evident in how the federal budget is allocated. And the budget process marches to its own inexorable beat. The Office of Management and Budget (OMB) had issued budget guidance, and within the next three months the budget would be signed, sealed, and delivered to Congress. Our best and perhaps only opportunity to make the case for additional funding was upon us.

The purpose of the meeting in the Tank was twofold. We needed to be absolutely sure about our analysis. There is no place for crying wolf in dealing with the White House and Congress on matters of budget. And we needed to provide recommendations on how to address the problem.

The Joint Chiefs were a tight-knit and battle-tested group when it came to the budget. We had been through a succession of very tough budget years in the aftermath of the 2008 recession, as well as the imposition of the 2011 Budget Control Act and its sequestration mechanism, which was triggered in 2013. For reasons best left to an explanation by economists, the effect of sequestration was felt most severely in readiness and modernization. For purposes of this story, suffice it to say that coming out of the 2013 sequestration, the Joint Chiefs were understandably more anxious than usual about the budget in 2014.

And so the Tank session quickly produced a consensus that we needed to communicate our concerns directly to the president with urgency. Concluding that in the previous year's budget negotiations we might not have adequately or persuasively articulated the real risk to national security, we decided to prepare a memorandum for the president outlining our concerns. And we decided we would all sign the memorandum, to ensure that both he and the secretary of defense appreciated that each of the services individually and the Joint Force as a whole would be adversely affected by the proposed defense budget. We agreed that I would draft the memorandum and provide it to each of them personally for signature, to minimize the risk of the memorandum leaking. It was a Friday. Our goal was to have the secretary of defense deliver it to the president the following Tuesday at a routinely scheduled weekly meeting.

On Monday I reviewed the memorandum with the secretary of defense. We all had a great deal of respect for Secretary Hagel. A Vietnam veteran, former senator, and former deputy at the Department of Veterans Affairs, he had a deep appreciation for the challenges we were facing after more than a decade of war, and he had an uncommon touch with soldiers, sailors, airmen, and marines. He listened patiently and then asked several insightful questions about our analysis and our assessment of risk. Once he was satisfied, he said he would take the memorandum to the president the next day. I explained to him that what I had just given him was the only signed copy and that we had gone to great lengths to ensure that our advice to him and the president would be protected.

On Tuesday afternoon I headed to Connecticut, where I was scheduled to give a lecture the next day at a leadership summit organized by the University of Connecticut's hall-of-fame women's basketball coach, Geno Auriemma. Coach Auriemma and I met for dinner on Tuesday night to go over the agenda.

Geno Auriemma is both a terrific basketball coach and an engaging, interesting dinner companion. He's got a great sense of humor and an incredible catalogue of stories from his time in coaching, both at the college level and with our women's Olympic basketball team. I was really enjoying our time together—until my BlackBerry buzzed at my hip. I glanced at the screen to see if I recognized the phone number. I did. It was the secretary of defense's office.

"Excuse me, Geno. I've got to take this call," I apologized as I stood up from the table and moved to a quiet corner of the room. "This is General Dempsey," I said into the phone.

"Please stand by for the secretary of defense," said a voice from the Pentagon.

"Hello, Marty." I recognized Secretary Hagel's voice.

"Hello, sir."

"Listen, Marty. I just came out of my meeting with the president, and I discussed your memorandum with him."

"Thanks, sir. How did it go?"

"Well, that's why I'm calling," he replied. "Not well. He doesn't understand what you're trying to accomplish with the memorandum. I think he may call you tonight."

"Okay, sir. Thanks for the heads-up. Any advice for when I speak to him?"

"No. I think you and the chiefs have valid concerns. I'm sure you'll be able to sort it out with him."

"All right, sir. I'll watch for the call and let you know how it goes." I returned to the table.

"Do we need to head for the basement?" Geno quipped.

"Thankfully not," I said. "Just some budget issues."

A few stories and one course of a three-course meal later, my BlackBerry buzzed again. I looked down: White House Communications Office.

"Sorry, Geno. Got to take this one too. Be right back."

"General Dempsey," I said into the phone.

"Stand by for the president."

Soon I heard President Obama's familiar voice on the other end of the line. "Marty," he began, "what are you trying to accomplish with this memorandum that Chuck Hagel delivered to me this afternoon?"

Uncharacteristically straight to the issue, I thought. I started to reply, but he continued.

"Listen, we've got some real problems with this year's budget, and this memorandum is not going to help me in solving them one bit. This is not the way I expect to get your advice, not the kind of loyalty I expect—"

"Sir, if I may—" I tried to interject. But I quickly realized it was premature.

The president went on for a full five minutes. It seemed even longer. He was clearly upset, but the only indication was a slightly elevated volume. For the first minute or so, I felt myself getting a little angry. *At some point I hope he gives me a chance to explain,* I thought. Gradually my anger gave way to begrudging admiration. *This is a first-class butt-chewing, and without even a single swear word.* But I knew I had to be ready to respond when he offered me the opportunity.

"You know the midterm elections are next week," he concluded. "Are you trying to box me in with this document?"

I snapped back into the moment. Had the president just suggested that the Joint Chiefs were using the midterm elections to manipulate him?

"Absolutely not, sir. I'm not even sure what you mean."

"Well, you know this memorandum will leak, and if my administration is portrayed as not supporting the military, it could affect the election," he shot back. "You're boxing me in."

Wow, I thought. It hadn't even occurred to us that our memorandum would be interpreted in the context of the midterm elections.

"Sir, the memorandum won't leak, and honestly we didn't even consider the midterm elections. Our motivation was exactly the opposite of boxing you in. We know that early next year we're going to have to testify before Congress about the budget. We all felt it was better that you hear our concerns now, when you can still do something about them. We were trying to *avoid* boxing you in."

There was a brief silence.

"Okay, Marty. What do you recommend we do at this point?"

"Sir, I suggest I bring the Joint Chiefs over to the White House to meet with you as soon as possible. We'll lay out our concerns. If we're persuasive, we'll ask you to reconsider the defense budget. If we're not persuasive, I expect you'll tell us to figure out how to live within the proposed numbers."

"Fair enough," the president replied. "We'll set it up for later this week."

"Thank you, sir. We'll be ready."

Back to the table. Geno looked at me.

"Okay," I said, "now we should head to the basement." We both laughed.

The meeting took place in the White House Situation Room later in the week. The president, national security adviser, White House chief of staff, and director of the OMB were all in attendance. Secretary Hagel was there too. The Joint Chiefs explained their concerns. The president and his team had several questions, which we answered. Then the president laid out a two-step process in which he would approve additional funding in the base budget once the OMB crunched the numbers. If there were still irreconcilable issues in the base budget, he said he would consider using the Other Contingency Operations (OCO) fund to bridge the gap. Working with the OMB over the next several weeks, we built a budget adequate for our national security needs. The president approved it.

The memorandum never leaked.

The process taught us some things about leading and advising, and also about loyalty.

We were right to have flagged our problem as soon as we recognized it. But what we saw as dutifully providing advice, an act of loyalty to the commander in chief, had been interpreted as exactly the opposite. That's because even the best advice must be sensitive to timing and competing priorities. For us, the budget had become a singularly important issue; for the president, it was one of several equally important issues. There would be other important issues we would have to resolve with him in the months ahead, and from that moment on, except in times of crisis, I would always seek the advice of the White House chief of staff about how to best time our interventions.

It had been an awkward moment but also an opportunity to gain an appreciation of how misperceptions can affect what should be a mutual understanding of loyalty. At that point, I was halfway through my time as the principal military adviser to the president. We would both benefit from that mutual understanding throughout my remaining time with him.

THE PHOTOGRAPH
WEST POINT, 2016

I had been retired from the Army for about six months when my phone rang in late April 2016. It was the superintendent of West Point, Lieutenant General Bob Caslen. I had known Bob since our days at West Point, where he was a year behind me. He had played center on the football team and still looked like he could step into that position again. He had multiple tours in Iraq and Afghanistan under his belt.

He had seen and done it all. A good friend and a man of utmost character, he was doing a great job at West Point. Three years in, many were calling him one of the best superintendents in Academy history.

"Sir," he said, "if you have a minute, I could use some advice."

"Sure, Bob. What's up?"

He told me that a couple of days earlier, a group of African American female senior cadets had taken a picture together in their dress uniforms on the steps of a historic West Point building. Such photos had become something of a tradition among cadets, but this particular group had posed with their arms raised and fists clenched. The picture had made its way onto social media and was beginning to create an uproar among some who thought that the cadets were making a political statement in support of Black Lives Matter.

"Well," I said, "obviously, part of our professional ethos is that we don't make political statements or gestures in uniform. Were they?"

"I don't know yet, sir. I've initiated an investigation to find that out. In the meantime, I was wondering if you have any advice about how much or how little we should be responding to the criticism. It's mostly on social media right now, but I'm sure it will be in the mainstream media soon. Do you have any advice?"

"Bob, I appreciate your confidence in me. What you need to know is that *I* have confidence in *you* that you'll do what's right, both for these cadets and for the Academy. The first thing I'd suggest is that whatever you do, do it quickly—thoroughly but quickly. Social media moves issues and swings attitudes at an unbelievable pace. Second, the investigation should tell you whether they were making an innocent gesture of solidarity or a purposeful political statement. You'll know what actions you should take at that point. Finally, you'll be criticized no matter what you do, so trust your instincts and stand by your decision."

Predictably, a debate about the photograph and the motivations behind it soon broke out in the mainstream media. There was no shortage of views on the subject expressed by pundits, alumni, and elected officials.

The investigation was completed in three days. Bob was transparent throughout and interviewed several of the young female cadets personally. In the end, he concluded that their gesture was an innocent expression of solidarity among sixteen women who were about to graduate together from an institution that is one of the most demanding in America—academically, physically, and in terms of leadership. Nevertheless, he counseled them about becoming more self-aware about their role and actions in a profession that must remain apolitical. With that, he declared the issue concluded.

His decision was welcomed by some but heatedly criticized by others. Those criticizing Bob Caslen attacked his character, his judgment, and his courage. They accused him of "political correctness" and of allowing the politicization of the military. They called for his removal as superintendent and for much sterner punishment for the cadets in the photograph. They questioned his loyalty to West Point.

Bob demonstrated confidence and composure throughout. He stood by his decision. At risk to his own reputation, he was loyal to the cadets entrusted to his care. It would have been easy, even understandable, for him to let the harsh criticism affect his decision. He did not.

Loyalty must be earned. Once earned, it must be nurtured and then earned again. For it to work, it must be equally important to those in leadership positions and to those who follow them.

Loyalty is an important but sometimes elusive intersection of timing, intentions, motivations, and communications. It almost always takes courage. It's a two-way street, and those traveling on each side must work diligently to avoid a collision.

CHAPTER FIVE

DON'T HURRY

BE QUICK, BUT DON'T HURRY
WEST POINT, 1970

I left my room, crossed the narrow dormitory hallway, and turned a sharp ninety degrees to my right, keeping my left shoulder close to the wall as I had been trained to do. The hallway was clear, so I started jogging toward the staircase. I was thinking I might still be able make it to class on time, avoiding the demerits that would be the consequence of a late arrival, when suddenly I heard the unmistakable voice of my cadet company commander.

"Mr. Dempsey," he called out. "What do you think you're doing?"

I froze in my tracks. He was behind me.

"I'm going to math class, sir."

I heard his footsteps approach, then stop just a few feet away.

"I assumed you were headed to class, Mr. Dempsey," he said in a calm but stern voice. "What I want to know is why you're running in my hallway."

"I'm late, sir."

"That's not my problem, Mr. Dempsey. It's yours. You are aware that plebes are expected to walk with a purpose, at approximately our parade pace of one hundred twenty steps per minute, and never to run unless told to do so."

"Yes, sir."

"These rules, Mr. Dempsey, are intended to instill order, discipline, and precision in new cadets. Your behavior right now suggests that you may have your own ideas about what's important."

"I understand, sir," I assured him. At this point I had resigned myself to being late to class and just wanted to survive this unpleasant encounter.

"I'm going to write up a fourth-class performance report on you, Mr. Dempsey. Perhaps next time you'll leave for class on time, and perhaps next time you won't compound your problem by failing to maintain control of yourself."

"Yes, sir," I replied. The adverse report would probably result in some kind of disciplinary action, but there wasn't much I could do about that now.

With that, he departed, and I headed toward class, walking with a purpose at the designated pace. Or maybe just a few beats faster. *Not sure I understand all this "walk with a purpose" stuff anyway,* I grumbled inwardly.

A few weeks later, I tried to walk on to West Point's basketball team. I had been a decent high school basketball player, so when I heard that Coach Bob Knight was looking for a few walk-ons to flesh out the freshman basketball team, I thought I'd give it a try.

I was well aware that my five-foot-ten, 140-pound frame was unlikely to make much of an impression on the coaches, so I decided to see if I could get noticed for my hustle on both offense and defense.

I was working hard on both ends of the court when Coach Knight abruptly halted the proceedings. He gathered me and twenty-five or so of my classmates at half-court. Coach Knight was an intimidating figure at an Academy filled with intimidating figures. He had accumulated a stellar record as West Point's basketball coach and would soon depart for Indiana University, where he would become one of the all-time great collegiate basketball coaches.

"Have any of you ever heard of legendary UCLA men's basketball coach John Wooden?" he asked.

"Yes, sir." We all nodded.

"Well, Coach Wooden has a saying: 'Be quick, but don't hurry.' Do any of you have any idea what he means by that?"

"Yes, sir," we chorused, nodding again. *Well, maybe,* I thought, *but I'm not about to ask him to clarify it.*

"Then why the hell don't you act like it?" he said. "I've never seen anything like what I'm seeing today. You're all running around like your damn hair is on fire. Do you think any of you at any point might find a way to play under control so I can figure out who the basketball players are among you?"

"Yes, sir." More nods.

At the end of the tryout, I was notified by an assistant coach that I didn't need to return the next day. I was disappointed, but it wasn't unexpected, and I was intrigued by Coach Knight's reference to the difference between being quick and being in a hurry. Sounded a lot like what the company commander had said to me.

Maybe there's something to this idea that we should always move at a pace we can control and sustain.

IN HOT PURSUIT OF THE ENEMY
GERMANY, 1975

My radio crackled. It was my platoon sergeant, reporting that the enemy was in retreat. As a cavalry platoon leader, I knew my job was to maintain contact with them. Behind my forty-man, twelve-vehicle platoon was a much larger formation of almost one hundred armored vehicles, prepared to maneuver through and around me and overwhelm the enemy. It would create real momentum for us and be a serious setback for the enemy, but not if I lost track of them. I reached for the microphone.

"Bravo 15," I barked, "this is Bravo 16. Don't lose contact with them. Continue to push forward. My section will tuck in behind you so we can move faster."

I could feel my vehicle picking up speed as the driver maneuvered to keep up with the platoon sergeant's vehicles in front of us. I made my report to the troop commander, telling him that we had temporarily lost contact with the retreating enemy but that we weren't far behind and would regain contact shortly. I sensed his excitement that we had the enemy in retreat, but his final instructions to me were to make sure my platoon stayed dispersed as we moved, so that we could support each other if we came upon anything unexpected.

I was in the tank commander's hatch of an M551 airborne armored assault vehicle. Known as the "General Sheridan," it had been designed for mobility in the jungles of Vietnam and had a short, powerful, smooth-bore 152-millimeter cannon. The Sheridan was light enough to be dropped by parachute from a C-130 cargo aircraft—once, at least, we often joked—but it could be an insufferable ride for everyone inside when moving quickly over rugged terrain. Terrain like we were moving over right now.

We were chewing up the fields, closing in on an enemy we imagined was desperately fleeing us. Because the Sheridan could float—although nobody I knew had ever been brave enough to actually try floating one—its exhaust was directed upward, giving it the appearance of a rooster tail. I gazed with satisfaction at the rooster tails of the five Sheridans in front of mine moving inexorably forward. Then I looked back at the map to orient myself and prepare to render a progress report to the troop commander.

A minute or so later, I looked up from the map, as much to relieve a brief wave of nausea from the rough ride as to see where we were. I immediately realized we weren't dispersed. At all. We had bunched up, we were in a straight line, and we were moving fast—much faster than I knew we should be.

I grabbed the radio and called the platoon sergeant, but he wasn't answering. These exercises were designed to introduce the kind of problems we could expect to face in real combat, and communications was always one of them. The "fog of war," we called it.

In the 1970s, the threat of a conflict between the United States and its NATO allies and the Soviet Union and its Warsaw Pact allies was real enough that each fall, after the crops in the local fields were harvested, U.S. forces stationed in Germany would stage extensive maneuvers. To make sure we could reinforce Europe in the event of a conflict, tens of thousands of soldiers and their equipment would also be shipped from the United States to Germany. This annual event was called Return of Forces to Germany (REFORGER). Lasting about a month, it was the culminating and by far the most important event in our training year.

REFORGER was a free-flowing exercise in that the two opposing forces maneuvered with few limitations. There were no scripted battles; skirmishes occurred when and where the two sides encountered each other. As a result, the tactical skills of leaders at every level were on display. Victory generally went to the side that could discern the enemy's intentions first, maneuver most effectively, bring the most firepower to bear, reorganize and resupply most quickly, and then continue the attack. Day and night for two weeks we fought on.

There were other more symbolic and political purposes of the REFORGER exercises. The interaction of the American, British, Canadian, and German forces was an important image to transmit to the Soviets on the other side of the border. But at the lower levels, it wasn't symbolic at all. It was very competitive.

These were the days before "laser tag" technology, so the adjudication of individual battles was left to umpires who traveled with opposing groups and judged which side had gained the advantage and inflicted the most damage. Vehicles indicated that they were "firing" their weapons by flashing their headlights.

My platoon was in hot pursuit of the enemy. We were moving east to west, with the Rhine River just ten or so kilometers ahead. The Rhine was the most significant natural barrier in these exercises, just as it had been during World War II. Getting across it would be a huge blow to the enemy and open the door to our objective, a small German town twenty kilometers beyond the opposite shore.

Bouncing along, it was almost impossible to read my map. There was no bridge over the Rhine to be seized in our sector, but the Army engineers behind me had a floating bridge they could emplace to get us across. I was about to contact my troop commander to ask where he wanted me to position the engineers, when suddenly the ride became unexpectedly smooth.

I looked up. We had moved out of the fields and were now on a paved road. *I can't imagine the enemy has left this road unguarded,* I thought. I began to worry.

"Bravo 15," I radioed, "this is Bravo 16. We need to slow down and spread out . . ." My voice trailed off.

We had just entered a large open field, several football fields in depth and width. Across the field, in the tree line, I could see more than a dozen flashing lights. We had found the retreating enemy—the hard way.

The umpires signaled for us to stop. The adjudication didn't go well. I had lost two thirds of my platoon. The enemy had lost almost nothing.

During the after-action review, which follows every training exercise, the umpire painstakingly described what had happened. In our zeal to regain contact with the enemy, we had moved too fast, without discipline, driven into an ambush, and lost any sense of the order necessary to support each other. *Other than that, we did well,* I thought wryly.

We were in a hurry, and we paid the price. The troop commander wasn't happy, but I consoled myself that it was a training exercise, and we had learned a valuable lesson.

CAMPAIGN AGAINST THE MAHDI ARMY
SOUTHERN IRAQ, 2004

At the beginning of April 2004, after a year in Iraq, Task Force Old Ironsides was ready to turn over responsibility for Baghdad to the 1st Cavalry Division and go home. However, April soon became the most violent month of the war in Iraq. By its end, we had been told that our tour of duty would be extended until an uprising by the Mahdi Army (the militant militia of radical cleric Moqtada al-Sadr in southern Iraq) could be subdued. The vast majority of the supplies for U.S. forces in Iraq were transported on the road leading from Kuwait through southern Iraq into Baghdad and beyond. That road had to remain open, and the militia was threatening it.

Uncertainty is the greatest threat to soldiers' morale. To give my soldiers and their families some idea of how much longer they'd be away from home, I told them it would likely take us 90 to 120 days to complete our new mission. I could sense their disappointment. Almost to a man they believed they could accomplish the mission sooner, but I cautioned them that it would be important not only to defeat the militia but to maintain the support of the civilian population as we conducted our operations. That meant we would have to be deliberate. It would take time.

And this wasn't a training mission. Fighting in Baghdad over the past year had cost us many lives. Fighting in southern Iraq over the next three months would cost us many more.

In preparing for our new mission, we identified three main pockets of militia resistance in southern Iraq: in Najaf, Kufa, and Karbala. Each of these cities had centuries-old shrines and religious significance within the Shia sect of Islam. Moreover, Najaf was the center of Shia political power in Iraq.

When he heard that we would remain in Iraq, Major General Jim Mattis called to ask me if I could take control of the area just south of Baghdad where he had several hundred marines. He needed them for the very tough fight he was then waging in Fallujah. I agreed, and so our new mission became controlling the area south of Baghdad *and* defeating the Shia militia in Najaf, Kufa, and Karbala.

Making the task more complicated, the fighters in the area just south of Baghdad—which our soldiers in combat there called the "Triangle of Death"—were Sunni fighters supporting their fellow Sunni insurgents in Fallujah. So our task was to gain control of four distinct geographic locations and fight two very different fights.

We estimated that we'd be facing 300 Sunni insurgents in South Baghdad and approximately 1,500 Shia militiamen in Najaf, Kufa, and Karbala. They were well armed and battle tested. They had also learned how to effectively hide among the local population, either by enlisting civilians' support or by intimidating them.

In planning the mission, it would be important to keep all of our activities synchronized. In executing the mission, it would be important to move at a pace we could control.

We knew it wouldn't do any good to defeat the militia in southern Iraq unless we could also find a way to separate the fighters from the population and give the people something to be hopeful about.

I had three brigade-sized units ready to move, each with approximately 2,500 soldiers. Each of them would have artillery, engineer, and rotary-wing helicopter support. To ensure that we could reach out to the leaders of the villages, towns, and tribes along the way, we requested and received support from the Coalition Provisional Authority, with civilian teams from our Department of State and the U.S. Agency for International Development (USAID). They would be our interlocutors with the population.

We had the mission. We had the resources. We began to move. Leaders at every level understood that our goal was to move inexorably but deliberately through southern Iraq, messaging local leaders and the militia constantly to make it clear to them that they had a choice: they could surrender their weapons and become part of the political contest that was taking place in Iraq or reject our outreach and fight.

Colonel Rob Baker's 2nd Brigade, 1st Armored Division would first occupy southern Baghdad to suppress the Sunni insurgents, prevent them from interfering in the Marines' fight in Fallujah, and shield us as we moved south. Our plan was for the rest of Task Force Old Ironsides to arrive on the outskirts of Kufa, Najaf, and Karbala simultaneously, so that the militia wouldn't have time to reposition forces to reinforce each other. Colonel Brad May's 2nd U.S. Cavalry would advance on Kufa and Najaf. Colonel Pete Mansoor's 1st Brigade, 1st Armored Division would advance on Karbala.

It was crucial that we remain aligned, which sometimes meant quickening our pace and at other times slowing it. There were roadside bombs, suicide bombers, downed bridges, cratered roads, and ambushes along the way. Our soldiers understood the importance of avoiding civilian casualties and reacted with discipline and precision. We marched on, fighting, repairing, and meeting with local political and religious leaders as the situation required.

As most of the task force moved south, Rob Baker kept the critical routes into Baghdad open in an intense fight where the Sunni insurgents—many of them foreign fighters—used dozens of suicide bombers. It quickly became clear why this part of Iraq had been nicknamed the Triangle of Death. In a single incident, we lost eight brave soldiers to a car bomb loaded with more explosives than we had seen in any other single incident.

When we arrived at the three cities in the south, it was apparent that some of the militia had faded away, hoping to live to fight another day, leaving a smaller but very determined and committed core of fighters who intended to stand and fight to the death. On the cities' outskirts, our advantages in intelligence, aerial surveillance, and airpower quickly overwhelmed them. Inside the cities, the fighting was intense, up close, and personal. As the most determined militia retreated to buildings near the sacred shrines, we had to patiently and precisely root them out without damaging the holy sites. To have done otherwise would have inflamed the population. Again, our soldiers acted with remarkable discipline.

In just over sixty days, we were able to report to the corps commander that we had accomplished our mission. The routes into Baghdad were open. The Shia militia had been suppressed. We turned over the area to other units, withdrew to Baghdad Airport, and prepared to go home.

Old Ironsides' campaign from April through June of 2004 obviously didn't end the war in Iraq. But it did keep us on track to restore sovereignty to the Iraqi people when the Coalition Provisional Authority was replaced in late June by an interim Iraqi government. It did draw Shia leaders back into the political arena for a time, although they would return to fighting several more times. And it did contribute to the Marines' success in the 2004 Battle of Fallujah, though there too future soldiers and marines would face further uprisings.

In the end, it highlighted the deep differences still dividing Iraq's Shia and Sunni populations and illuminated the interference of fighters from other countries, who flowed into Iraq to attempt to tip the military and political balance. After this campaign, everyone—in Iraq and in Washington—began talking about the U.S. mission in Iraq lasting years, not months as some had been suggesting.

For the leadership team of Task Force Old Ironsides, it was the way our soldiers accomplished their mission that was most impressive: Their resolve in staying focused when their deployment was extended. Their discipline, patience, and precision in execution. Their sacrifice and the sacrifice of their families.

Old Ironsides was quick, but we didn't hurry.

ISIS THREATENS IRBIL
NORTHERN IRAQ, 2014

I was the last one into the president's limousine, nicknamed "the Beast," so I reached back to pull the door closed behind me. I gave it a good tug, but it barely moved.

"Let me get that for you, sir," said the smiling Secret Service agent.

About an hour earlier, I had been sitting in the second row in the State Department's main conference room. The president was ten seats to my right, at the center of a large oval table. Around him sat forty African heads of state, some in suits, some in traditional tribal garb. It was an impressive sight. The August 2014 Africa Summit, more than a year in the planning, had been a great success. I could see from the president's demeanor that he was pleased.

To my immediate right sat Ambassador Susan Rice, the national security adviser, and to her right Ambassador Samantha Power, U.S. ambassador to the United Nations. They had been proponents of greater engagement in Africa for as long as I had known them—more than ten years in Rice's case—and this summit was clearly intended to be an important part of President Obama's legacy. I could tell that they too were very happy with its outcomes. Ambassador Power passed me a note: "When can we get together and discuss delivering on the commitments the president has made today?"

I was crafting my reply when I noticed one of Ambassador Rice's assistants and my aide-de-camp approaching behind us. Her assistant handed her a message. She quickly read it and passed it to me. It read: "ISIS on the move from Mosul toward Irbil. U.S. consulate preparing to evacuate." She asked me to meet her outside the conference room in ten minutes. My aide handed me a message: "General Austin is at his headquarters at Central Command. He needs to talk to you ASAP."

I knew I needed to call General Lloyd Austin first. We had largely withdrawn from Iraq in late 2011, when he was our commander there. Our remaining presence was limited to the areas around the U.S. embassy in Baghdad and the U.S. consulate in Irbil. He would know the implications of an ISIS assault on Irbil.

General Austin was as unflappable and precise as anyone we had in uniform. He got right to the point.

"Chairman, a convoy of fifty to seventy-five ISIS vehicles is moving toward Irbil. They're carrying probably three hundred to four hundred fighters with both light and medium-weight weapons. The Peshmerga"—these were Kurdish military forces—"are organizing to hold them at the Zab River, approximately one hundred kilometers west of Irbil. ISIS will be at the Zab within the next two hours. If they break through that line, there's not much between them and Irbil."

"What do you recommend, Lloyd?"

"We need to provide air support to the Pesh, Chairman. They're not going to be able to hold without it. If not, we should begin the evacuation of the consulate in Irbil immediately."

"Okay, Lloyd. We're with the president now. I'll brief him and be back to you soon. In the meantime, alert and prepare whatever assets you'll need to execute whichever course the president chooses."

After a short conversation with Ambassador Rice, she told me that I would ride with the president back to the White House in his limousine and brief him on what we knew. Once we arrived, he would assemble his national security team to discuss our options.

I called my executive officer back at the Pentagon. I needed the Joint Staff operations officer to prepare two slides for me to use in my discussion with the president: one on the resources available, including the specifics of air support for the Peshmerga, and one with the particulars of a possible evacuation of the hundred or so Americans at the U.S. consulate. I also instructed him to send me a map of northern Iraq. "I need someone to meet me at the West Wing entrance with these materials in forty-five minutes," I told him.

I could see the president bidding farewell to the African leaders as he worked his way out of the conference room. I knew I had just a few minutes before he would make his exit and head for the limousine.

Slow down, I reminded myself. *Be quick, but don't hurry.* I knew that the embassy staff in Iraq would be looking for a rapid response. I also knew that once this issue gained the attention of the media, the pressure for action would rapidly mount. But there were things we needed to know before rushing headlong into this unknown and rapidly changing situation.

As I walked toward the president's limousine, I wondered if this coming battle was anywhere near the site of the Battle of Gaugamela, between Alexander the Great and the Persian king Darius III in the third century BC. *Twenty-three hundred years of history working against us in that part of the world,* I reminded myself.

Once the door of the Beast closed, I took a look around and buckled my seat belt. It was a massive vehicle, at least ten tons, and it felt like it. I settled in next to the president as Ambassador Rice, sitting across from me, prepared to take notes.

"What have we got, Marty?"

"Mr. President, the U.S. consulate in Irbil is at risk." I explained what we knew and previewed the decision I would be seeking back at the White House.

The president was quiet. "I see," he said. "Sounds like we don't have any good options."

"No, sir. And things are moving fast."

"Well, at some point will someone please explain how a bunch of mercenaries in Toyota pickup trucks are overrunning the Iraqi army we've spent the last eleven years building? And how is it possible that they were that fragile and we didn't see it?" He was frustrated. Understandably so.

"Fair question, sir, and we'll work on that as soon as we resolve this situation in Irbil," I replied. *Eleven years of history in this war to overcome,* I reminded myself. He didn't say much more for the remainder of the short trip.

In fact, there had been signs of impending trouble in Iraq, both within the Iraqi military and in Iraqi politics. CENTCOM had been concerned for some time. With no military presence anywhere in Iraq except in Baghdad and at the consulate in Irbil, we had no eyes, no ears, and few relationships. Even so, we had been tracking several weak signals, the kind that sometimes get overlooked as they accumulate over time.

The Iraqi prime minister had slowly but surely replaced the most capable army commanders with much less capable men he knew would be loyal to him. He had tacitly supported his Shia political supporters as they manipulated army recruiting, effectively losing any semblance of balance among Shia, Sunni, and Kurds. Now the Iraqi army was dominated by Shia soldiers. The best equipment was given to Shia units. Payroll was distributed most reliably to Shia units. The few units in the army with Sunni representation—but under Shia leadership—were in the north, where ISIS was now over-running them.

As one Sunni politician in Baghdad later explained to me, "the Sunni soldiers in northern Iraq know they don't have the support of the government in Baghdad, so they aren't prepared to die for them."

But these discussions would be for another day. We had an immediate and far more time-sensitive problem on our hands.

At the White House, I proceeded to the West Wing entrance to meet the staff officer sent over from the Pentagon with the briefing materials. I had ten minutes before I had to be in the Oval Office, so I called my operations officer, Army lieutenant general Bill Mayville. Bill was an extraordinary operations officer—thoughtful and thorough, a combat-tested warrior. He really knew the business and had the trust and confidence of all the services. Not surprisingly, he had anticipated everything I would need for my discussion with the president.

Meanwhile, the CENTCOM team had begun identifying and alerting the resources we would need to support whatever decision the president made. They had ISR (intelligence, surveillance, and reconnaissance) en route, aerial refueling aircraft prepared to launch, strike aircraft identified and being re-missioned, and a combat search-and-rescue team alerted, for use in the event of a downed pilot. They also had a C-17 cargo plane preparing, in case the decision was made to evacuate the consulate.

Lloyd Austin was a seasoned leader who knew that even in a crisis we had to move deliberately, or a bad situation could quickly turn worse. He didn't yet have ISR overhead to provide images of the forces converging near Irbil, and he knew that the situation on the ground would be ambiguous at best and probably intensely confusing. ISIS had stopped flying their identifying black flags weeks ago, so it would be important to gain a clear picture of who was friend and who was foe before we began dropping bombs. He had his CENTCOM team moving quickly but making sure they kept building their knowledge and adapting as they acted.

"The ISIS advance has slowed a bit, sir, and the Peshmerga are getting organized along the river," Bill reported. "We have a little more time than we initially thought—maybe four hours more—but it is our assessment that a decision to provide close air support to the Kurds and an announcement of our intention to do so would stiffen their defenses even before the aircraft arrive."

"Thanks, Bill," I said. "I'll want to meet with you and do a VTC with General Austin when I get back to the Pentagon. Please set it up."

The national security team had gathered in the Oval Office by the time I arrived: the president, vice president, deputy secretary of state, national security adviser, and several representatives of the intelligence community. The secretary of defense was traveling overseas but was being kept abreast of the situation.

It had been nearly three years since we had last used force in Iraq. The decision to use force now would open a new phase in the conflict against ISIS and mean renewed commitments in Iraq and probably Syria.

Three years of history to overcome, I reminded myself.

I walked over to a position behind the president's and vice president's seats. I handed the president a two-by-two-foot map of northern Iraq and leaned over between them, using my pen as a pointer.

"Mr. President," I began, "at the end of my briefing I will ask for your permission to begin employing combat and support aircraft either to attack ISIS west of the Zab River or to evacuate the U.S. consulate in Irbil. I am prepared to discuss how we would accomplish either of these missions, the opportunity costs elsewhere in the region, and the risk to our pilots."

The president listened carefully to the briefing. At one point, he instructed his staff to get our ambassador to Iraq on the phone so he could get his insights on how the Iraqi prime minster and parliament were dealing with the crisis in the north. They were panicked, he learned, and quite unsure about what to do.

Several times the president asked how confident we were that the Kurds could hold along the Zab River, even with our assistance. He asked whether we had the intelligence necessary to use airpower without risk to civilians in the area and whether the commitment of U.S. airpower might eventually lead to a request from the Iraqi government for additional U.S. ground forces. He asked for our assessment of what ISIS would do once they were turned back from Irbil.

When he had all the information available, he leaned back in his chair, looked around the room, and asked for my recommendation.

I knew that the prospect of using airpower against this particular ISIS threat near Irbil was not the thing that weighed most heavily in the president's thinking. The prospect of becoming involved in a protracted fight against ISIS that would likely include additional U.S. ground forces was what weighed most heavily on him. So I decided to ask for only what I needed in the moment. The president knew we would be thinking ahead, and we could address future requirements later.

"Sir," I said, "I recommend that we use our airpower to attack ISIS in support of the Peshmerga along the Zab River. Our loss of prestige and influence in Iraq will be significant if we're forced to evacuate our consulate in Irbil. Moreover, given the report we just heard from our ambassador in Baghdad, I'm not sure what will stop ISIS at this point, unless we stop them here."

He looked around the room at his other advisers. They all nodded in agreement.

A few minutes later the president made the decision to commit U.S. airpower to the defense of Irbil. He instructed me to prepare a recommendation within the next forty-eight hours for an extended air campaign to keep pressure on ISIS throughout Iraq and an assessment of what ground forces we might need in Irbil and Baghdad to protect U.S. personnel and facilities, including the embassy and the airport. He told his staff to schedule a press conference the next day to explain his actions to the American people. He instructed his congressional liaison to brief the chairmen of the armed services, intelligence, and foreign affairs committees.

At CENTCOM headquarters in Tampa, Lloyd Austin continued to calmly assemble the pieces in anticipation of the president's decision. Lloyd knew that, with the decision made, there would be an immediate and almost insatiable appetite for information about conditions in Mosul and Irbil, so he began reaching out to the intelligence resources across our government and in Iraq. Because the mission would be an intricate collaboration among the Army, Navy, and Air Force, he carefully and deliberately identified objectives, clarified command relationships, and established time lines.

The combatant commanders and I had a long-standing agreement that they would always act within their authorities to get things done, and we would discuss it later. Each of us lived by Jack Welch's motto "Only make the decisions that only you can make." As a result, Lloyd was ready by the time he received the president's decision. Soon U.S. combat aircraft were on station and attacking ISIS forces west of the Zab River. The introduction of U.S. aircraft buoyed the Kurds' confidence, and they began pushing ISIS back toward Mosul. Eventually the lines would stalemate around Mosul, remaining there for many months while the Iraqi army recovered from its defeat. But ISIS had reached its geographic limits.

Our efforts were not without moments of high drama and mind-numbing frustration. Mistrust within the Iraqi government had never been higher, and although we were clearly acting on their behalf, they were not the least bit reluctant to question our motives as we began to reintroduce resources into the country.

Soon after authorizing the flow of unmanned aerial vehicles (UAVs) from the Gulf into northern Iraq to get eyes on ISIS, I received word that the Iraqi government had filed an official complaint with the U.S. embassy in Baghdad, stating that one of our UAVs had flown too close to the holy shrine at Najaf as it moved north. I knew this would be the work of Shia militia leaders, eager to make sure that Iraq's prime minister didn't get too close to his U.S. advisers.

"How close was the UAV to the shrine at its closest point during the transit?" I asked the young major briefing me on the incident.

"Approximately ten kilometers, sir."

"Are you kidding me?"

"No, sir. Ten kilometers."

I was really annoyed.

"Okay. Please ask the embassy to let the Iraqi prime minister know that our UAV was nowhere near the shrine as it transited north, and that unless he demonstrates some trust in us, he should prepare to greet ISIS at the gates of Baghdad."

I never found out whether that message was delivered with the intensity I intended, but we didn't have much interference from Iraq's political leaders after that until ISIS was contained within Mosul.

In many ways, the battle along the Zab was the turning point in the fight against ISIS. It would take time to break their hold in northern Iraq and Syria. The U.S. commitment to the fight against ISIS would grow. And, of course, Iraqi politics and the lingering mistrust among Sunni, Shia, and Kurds would complicate and slow progress.

Nevertheless, defeating ISIS was—and continues to be—a case study in why it's important not to hurry. It suggests that "not hurrying" requires us to learn how to ask the right questions at the right time. It suggests that even—perhaps especially—in the midst of a crisis we should allow leaders at every level to execute their judgment and discretion in solving problems, freeing up the most senior leaders to focus on making the decisions that only they can make.

☆ ☆ ☆ ☆

Not hurrying is a learned instinct, a felt instinct, an important attribute for everyone to understand.

CHAPTER SIX

WELCOME MOMENTS OF SURPRISING CLARITY

ICE BLOCKS ON THE HUDSON
WEST POINT, 1971

There's no place as beautiful as West Point in the spring, summer, and fall and no place as dismal as West Point in January and February. In fact, cadets commonly refer to this time of year at the Academy as "gloom period."

This particular day in February 1971 was overcast, windy, and bitterly cold. I had the collar of my cadet overcoat turned up, but even the heavy wool, three-quarter-length coat was no match for the wind. *At least it's at my back,* I thought. As I walked from my barracks room to the cemetery, I took note of the ice blocks floating in the Hudson River.

It was unusual for a plebe to be excused from class for any reason. But I had asked to attend the funeral and interment of an Army captain recently killed in action in Vietnam. He was a graduate of the West Point Class of 1964, and I had met him once, several years earlier. As I walked, I thought back on that day. . . .

"Marty, mind the store. I'm stepping outside for a moment," Mr. Martin called back to me. I was huddled over the large basin, busily scrubbing dishes. It was the summer of 1968, and I was the dishwasher and sometime busboy at the Lake Diner in Greenwood Lake, New York.

"Got it, sir. I'll be right out."

Greenwood Lake was a small vacation spot and bedroom community for New York City. Right in the middle of Main Street, the Lake Diner was an old 1950s-style, silver, subway-car-looking gathering spot for locals, who had chosen it as their sanctuary to escape the summer vacationers. I was a sophomore in high school. Mr. Martin and his co-owner and brother-in-law, Mr. Mullin, had hired me to work five days a week during the summer and several hours on weekends during the school year.

I usually ended up on Mr. Martin's shift. Initially I found him somewhat brusque, but gradually I became quite fond of him and his eccentricities. One day, when the diner was quiet, he educated me for about an hour on the fine art of tuning the transistor radio—once white but now yellowed—that he kept on a shelf near the griddle. "I have an ear for precision," he told me, carefully turning the dial with only the first three fingers on his right hand. I was just happy to get a break from dishwashing.

Because the Lake Diner was the locals' gathering place, I overheard pretty much all of the town's business—the real, the imagined, and the rumored. Mr. Martin would often encourage the conversation away from local issues to more national topics. He was very well read and had an insatiable appetite for news. The transistor radio was always tuned to his favorite news station. The only time I could change the channel to listen to music or sports was when he stepped out of the diner occasionally. I'd switch it back to the news before he returned, but he'd always know that I'd changed it. I never did master the fine art of tuning that radio.

When I came out of the kitchen on this day, I noticed Mr. Martin, Mr. Mullin, and a group of their family standing in front of the diner. They were obviously waiting for something, and soon the bus from

New York City pulled up at the stop across the street. As I watched, the passengers began to disembark, among them a young man in an Army uniform. I couldn't tell his rank, but I could see that he cut a striking figure, handsome, tan, and fit. He quickly crossed the street, and Mr. Mullin's daughter Nancy rushed to embrace him. I stepped back a bit from the window, feeling like I was intruding on a private family moment.

There were hugs all around as the entire Mullin-Martin family greeted him. Not long after, Mr. Martin led him inside and introduced us. I learned that he was Captain John Graham, West Point class of 1964, married to Mr. Mullin's daughter Nancy, and they had a two-year-old son. He was returning from a tour of duty in Vietnam. He and his family were happy beyond description.

Now I was walking to his funeral. In 1970 he had returned to Vietnam, and he was killed in action on January 16, 1971.

Even though I was at West Point, even though some of my classmates had served in Vietnam, and even though the West Point faculty was filled with Vietnam veterans, everything about the Vietnam War had been abstract to me until this moment.

When I got to the funeral, I greeted the family—those I knew and those I didn't know. It was heart-wrenching. I learned that Captain Graham had been nominated for the Silver Star, our nation's third-highest award for valor (which he would eventually receive). I watched his widow trying to be stoic when that was the last thing she wanted to be. I watched their five-year-old son and wondered how he could possibly understand what was happening around him.

After the interment, I headed back to the barracks. It was even colder walking back, as now I was facing into the wind. I noticed that the flow of ice on the river had reversed directions. It did that at this point, where the Hudson River turned west and the tide changed fifty miles to the south in New York Harbor. Still, on this day it had a strange feeling to it.

It was time to be a plebe again, but I knew I wouldn't be the same plebe I had been when I began my walk to the cemetery that day.

I thought back to my first day at West Point, seven months earlier..

My father and siblings drove me to West Point for R-Day, or Reception Day. You can't bring very much to West Point; every new cadet is allowed just a single bag containing personal items when they enter the Academy. I grabbed mine out of the trunk, hugged my family good-bye, and walked as confidently as possible toward the designated entry point. There I met the "Man in the Red Sash."

The Man in the Red Sash is West Point's answer to a welcoming committee. He—or, now, she—is literally a senior cadet in a white shirt over gray trousers with a red sash around his waist so that he can be identified by the new cadets trying to find their way into the maze of imposing Gothic buildings that is West Point.

I approached the Man in the Red Sash cheerfully. There were four new cadets in front of me, so I took my place in line, where I was told by another upper-class cadet to affix a tag to my trousers with my name on it.

"New Cadet Candidate Dempsey. Turn away from the Man in the Red Sash, stand erect, remain quiet, and keep your eyes to the front," I was told.

Behind me I could hear the other new cadets proceeding one by one to meet the Man in the Red Sash. I couldn't tell what they were talking about, but soon it was my turn.

I turned.

"New Cadet Candidate Dempsey, drop your bag."

I placed my bag on the ground next to me.

"New Cadet Candidate Dempsey, pick up your bag."

I picked up my bag.

"New Cadet Candidate Dempsey, drop your bag."

I placed my bag on the ground next to me, wondering what this self-absorbed control freak of a cadet was trying to get me to do.

"New Cadet Candidate Dempsey, pick up your bag."

Here we go again, I thought. This time was different.

"New Cadet Candidate Dempsey, you are one of the dumbest new cadet candidates that have come through my station today. I did not tell you to *place* your bag on the ground. I told you to *drop* your bag. There is an important difference. It is my conclusion that you are too dense to understand the difference and that therefore there is no way you will make it here at West Point. However, if you choose to continue to try and make it here, then pick up your bag and follow my instructions to the letter."

I have entered the twilight zone of the literal, I thought to myself. But I wasn't going to allow this first encounter to defeat me. I picked up my bag.

"New Cadet Candidate Dempsey, drop your bag," he barked.

I dropped my bag.

"Very good, New Cadet Candidate Dempsey. It only took you three tries to follow my instructions."

There followed a recitation by my tormentor of an impossible litany of tasks that I had to accomplish in the next four hours, before I and my fellow new cadet candidates would march onto the parade field and take the oath of office as new cadets in the United States Military Academy.

Now, looking out over the river after the funeral, I reflected ruefully, *From trying to understand something as simple as dropping my bag to trying to understand something as incomprehensible as being killed in action—in just seven months.*

An unsettling moment. As most surprisingly clarifying moments can be.

I picked up my pace and headed off to class.

LEADING UP
U.S. CENTRAL COMMAND, 2008

I was happily watching our one-year-old granddaughter, Kayla, playing in the sand, and shooing away the occasional hungry seagull, when I felt my BlackBerry vibrate. I glanced at the number on the screen and recognized it as my executive officer. I decided to let it go to voicemail.

We were on the beach in St. Petersburg, Florida. I was the three-star deputy commanding general of U.S. Central Command, but on this Monday morning I was playing the important role of Papa. My boss, Admiral Bill Fallon, had left the night before on a week-long visit to our troops in the Middle East. So I told the chief of staff, a superb Marine two-star named Tango Moore, that I was taking off for the day and he should call me only in an emergency. Central Command is the epicenter of the nation's war on terror, but my boss was on his way there, Tango was at headquarters, and I hadn't had a day off in more than a month. I knew that if something really important came up, I'd hear from Tango.

Two minutes later, my BlackBerry vibrated again. This time it was Tango. I walked a short distance down the beach.

"Hello, Tango," I said. "This better be important."

Tango and I had become very close, and he had a great sense of humor.

"Well, sir," he began, "I'm sorry to bother you, but I thought you should know that at fifteen hundred hours today the secretary of defense will announce that Admiral Fallon has decided to retire immediately, and you'll be named the acting commanding general of Central Command."

What a prankster, I thought.

"Is that so, Tango?" I replied. "Well, let's alert the Air Force that I'll need an aircraft this afternoon to take me up to Washington to see the secretary. Now, what do you really want?"

"You don't have to go up to see him, sir. But he would like to talk to you on the phone as soon as possible."

It dawned on me that he wasn't kidding.

"You're not kidding, are you?"

"No, sir, I'm not. I'm in the process of preparing the staff to brief you later today on how we'll reorganize to account for your transition into the role of commander."

"Okay, Tango. We'll pack up here and head back. I'll be there in about ninety minutes. Please let the SECDEF's office know I'll be calling then. And thanks for starting to get everything organized back there. The only reason I'm not in a panic right now is you."

As I walked back to our group on the beach, Deanie was glowering at me. "Don't tell me we have to go back to Tampa," she said.

"We do. In about three hours, I'm going to be the commander of CENTCOM," I told her.

"*What?*"

"I'll tell you about it on the way."

"Okay, I guess that's a pretty good reason to cut short our time at the beach. But"—she smiled—"we're stopping to get Kayla the ice cream we promised her."

Seven months earlier, in August 2007, I had been made the deputy commander of U.S. Central Command, headquartered in Tampa, Florida. It was a good fit for me after spending three of the past four years in Iraq. At the time, CENTCOM's area of responsibility included twenty-seven countries, from Pakistan in the east to Ethiopia in the west. It included most of South Asia, the Arabian Peninsula, the Gulf states, and the Horn of Africa.

With Admiral Fallon's retirement, I was now responsible for coordinating the activities of all of our Army, Navy, Air Force, and Marine forces in the CENTCOM area, as well as integrating the efforts of our allies and ensuring that our efforts were aligned with U.S. national security strategy and the intent of the secretary of defense.

Among the CENTCOM commanding general's many duties was the submission of a weekly report to the secretary of defense. This was typically a five- or six-page Word document, occasionally augmented with a few PowerPoint slides. It had always struck me as too long— and mostly an exercise in making sure the SECDEF knew we were working hard. We were, but I suspected that the SECDEF already knew that. Now that I was the commander, I wanted to change the report's format and intent.

Not surprisingly, the CENTCOM staff, the Joint Staff, and the SECDEF's staff were wary of any changes to the report. As far as anyone knew, everyone liked it the way it was. Nevertheless, as the "acting" commander, I decided to take my chances and direct the change anyway. The staff would still provide the underlying data, but I would write the report and submit it myself to the secretary of defense and the Chairman of the Joint Chiefs of Staff. To make it manageable and (I hoped) useful, I intended to limit it to two pages.

My first in-person meeting with Secretary of Defense Robert Gates was scheduled for a little more than a month after I began submitting my abbreviated weekly reports. My staff and I were there to brief him on one of our standing war plans. When we arrived in his conference room, we all waited at our designated places. When the SECDEF entered the room, we took our seats.

I expected that he would open the meeting with a few remarks. He did.

"General Dempsey, thanks for making the trek up here to Washington from Tampa. We're all interested in your thoughts about how the war plan we're about to discuss should evolve over time. But before we begin, I want to compliment you and your staff on the adaptation you've made to your weekly reports. They are clear and concise, and I can't tell you how much I appreciate clear and concise here in Washington, DC."

"Thank you, sir," I replied. "We all want to make sure we provide a product that's useful to you."

"Okay. Let's discuss this war plan," he said, opening his briefing book.

The briefing went well. Secretary Gates was a voracious reader, and he had obviously absorbed all the material provided to him in advance. After we received his guidance, he stood up and began to make his way to the door.

"Marty," he called out, "would you stick around a minute and join me in my office?"

"Of course, sir."

In his office, Secretary Gates offered me a seat at one of his two conference tables. He asked if I wanted a cup of coffee or a glass of water. I declined. Then he got down to business.

"How's it going over there?" he asked.

I knew he was referring to Afghanistan, where we had just increased our troop strength.

"Too soon to tell, sir," I replied. "We can push back the Taliban and continue the development of the Afghan National Security Forces, but unless the various ethnic groups and tribes find a way to cooperate and share power, I'm not sure it's going to make a lasting difference."

"I agree," he said. "We constantly make that point, both here and with NATO."

"Yes, sir." I nodded in agreement.

"Listen, I just want to reinforce again what I said in the conference room," he continued. "I really appreciate the way you communicate with me. In particular, I appreciate how you not only describe our current situation but always include your advice on what we should do next. You may think I have all the answers up here, but I assure you I do not. Keep it up."

"Thanks, sir," I said. "I will."

I departed the SECDEF's office shortly thereafter. On the long walk back through the Pentagon to meet my driver, I thought about what he had said.

A few years before that conversation, as a young brigadier general, I had taken a leader development course. One of its learning objectives was the idea of "leading up."

The course was intended to overcome the troubling tendency of high-performing junior leaders to become much less effective as senior leaders. The Army's research suggested that early in leaders' careers, we were overemphasizing their responsibility to "focus down" on those they were leading, to the point that anything else was considered self-serving, very nearly a dereliction of duty. The course was designed to help leaders make the transition from junior to senior leadership by understanding their responsibility to "lead down," "lead laterally," and "lead up" as situations required.

At the time, I thought I understood what it meant to "lead up," but I was wrong. It wasn't until my time as the acting commander of CENTCOM that I really understood the meaning and importance of "leading up."

Leading up means being attuned to the challenges of those serving above you. It means working to be clear and concise. It means giving advice that might stretch beyond your current responsibilities. It means being honest and humble.

My conversation with the SECDEF about what he looked for in those serving him was a memorable moment that would serve me well during the remainder of my career.

FIDDLERS ON THE ROOF
TEL AVIV, 2012

A big part of the job of the Chairman of the Joint Chiefs of Staff is building relationships with our military counterparts—some of whom are allies and some of whom are potential adversaries—around the world. I traveled to visit them in their countries, and they traveled to visit me in Washington, DC.

Because I had to be available to talk with both the secretary of defense and the president at any given moment, I traveled on an Air Force plane with secure communications equipment. It was usually a military version of the 757, painted white over blue and dubbed "Air Force Two" when the vice president was aboard. Across the length of the aircraft was emblazoned "United States of America." Whenever we landed anywhere, a large staircase would be wheeled into place and a greeting party would assemble at its foot. It was all very ceremonial, but as I descended, I always paused halfway down, looked back at those words on the aircraft, and reminded myself of my responsibilities to my country during the visit.

Some places I visited more frequently, in particular our long-standing allies and partners. One of those was Israel.

In 2012 I came down the stairs of my aircraft with Deanie for our first visit to Israel. Waiting at the bottom of the stairs were the chief of the Israel Defense Forces, Lieutenant General Benny Gantz, and his wife, Revital. We were acquainted, but this was our first meeting in our current roles.

"Good to see you again, Martin and Deanie," he said.

"Good to see you too, Benny. Hi, Revi," I replied. Hands were shaken all around.

We had a very full agenda. These visits were always somewhat rushed, as I didn't like to be away from Washington for very long. Nevertheless, they were important, and I always learned something from them.

The four of us chatted on the way to our waiting vehicles. Benny explained that we would briefly part company, allowing me and Deanie to freshen up at our hotel, and then we would meet for dinner at a place he had arranged.

We were in Tel Aviv, Israel's most populous city, situated on its Mediterranean coast. Just north of the ancient port city of Jaffa and just south of where Israel narrows to only nine miles wide, it is the home of Israel's Ministry of Defense and the headquarters of the Israel Defense Forces. With a police escort, Deanie and I traveled to our hotel and checked in. Two hours later, we were back on the move to meet Benny and Revi.

As we got into the car for the ride to dinner, my executive officer explained that we would be meeting them at Moshe Aviv Tower, at the time the tallest building in Tel Aviv. He didn't know anything more than that.

Benny was a graduate of our National Defense University and had served as a military attaché in the Israeli embassy in Washington, DC, so both he and Revi were fluent in English. And we all knew there was plenty to talk about. The Middle East was in turmoil, and Israel was becoming increasingly concerned about a proliferation of guided missiles and rockets in the hands of Hezbollah, Iran's surrogate in Lebanon. The next day at his headquarters, we would be talking about enhancing U.S. missile-defense cooperation with Israel.

As we pulled up to Moshe Aviv Tower, I thought about the complexity of the security situation in Israel. I wondered how Benny would help me understand it.

One of Benny's assistants met us at the car and guided us to the elevator. Sixty-five stories later, we stepped out and walked a short distance over to a staircase. The assistant explained that we were going up to the roof to meet Benny and Revi and then would return to the sixty-fifth floor for a catered dinner. Sounded interesting.

The roof of Moshe Aviv Tower is also a helipad. When we reached it, we found Benny and Revi standing next to a portable bar that had been set up for the occasion. Off to the right, I took note of several Israeli soldiers—who apparently were also musicians, as they stood holding violins at their sides.

Walking toward Benny and Revi, I took in the view from this vantage point. The sun had set, and the lights of the city and its suburbs were visible in every direction.

"Well, Benny," I said, "I must say this is a pleasant surprise."

"We enjoy this view, Martin. Let's have a glass of wine, and I'll tell you more about it."

"Sounds like an excellent idea, Benny." Israeli wine is very good.

Once the glasses of wine were in hand, we strolled for a bit around the helipad. Benny pointed out Old Jaffa south of us and the expanse of the Mediterranean to the west. He pointed north toward Lebanon, four hundred kilometers in the distance, and east toward Jerusalem, seventy kilometers away.

Finally, he stopped and asked me to do something for him.

"Martin, if you wouldn't mind, please turn slowly around in a circle and look at the density of the lights in almost every direction."

I did so.

"What you've just seen," he continued, "is forty-five percent of the population of the State of Israel. And in that direction"—he pointed to the north—"are one hundred thousand guided rockets and missiles in the hands of Hezbollah. That's the urgency of what we need to talk about tomorrow."

"Benny," I replied somberly, "I now understand your challenge much better."

And I did. It was a moment I wouldn't forget. It's important—vital, actually—to make the effort to understand the history, the interests, the hopes, and the fears of others if you hope to deal constructively with them and have a good relationship. It's important to learn and to broaden your perspective, to take advantage of memorable moments to *get out of yourself.*

I told Benny that I hoped he would share what he knew of the Palestinians' perspectives about their security as we drove from Tel Aviv to Jerusalem the next day. He readily agreed that a better under-standing of both sides of the issues was essential. I assumed we were ready to head downstairs for dinner.

"I have one more surprise for you, Martin," Benny said.

With that, he turned and gestured to the three Israeli soldiers standing nearby with their violins. They began to play. It was the theme song from *Fiddler on the Roof*—naturally.

When they were done, we applauded and made our way to dinner.

There were many other memorable, clarifying moments in my travels as chairman. A few were more surprising and thought-provok-ing than others.

THE DEMILITARIZED ZONE
BETWEEN NORTH AND SOUTH KOREA.

As I toured the conference building straddling the border between North and South Korea in what is known as the Joint Security Area (JSA), I made eye contact with the North Korean soldier standing outside the window on his side of the border. He was staring in at me. We were no more than five feet apart. What I expected to see in his eyes was unemotional, stoic resolve. What I saw was unmistakable hatred.

CHAPULTEPEC CASTLE.

Located in the center of Mexico City, Chapultepec Castle is home to Mexico's National Museum of History. On September 13, 1847, the Niños Héroes of Mexico's military academy died defending the castle from American soldiers during the Mexican-American War. A huge mural on the ceiling above the castle's main entrance honors these "child heroes." It portrays one of them, wrapped in the Mexican flag, leaping to his death from the castle walls rather than be captured by the Americans. As I stood gazing up at the mural, I was unsettled by the image of the young boy falling down upon me. In the background, peering down from the parapet of the castle at the falling boy, was the image of a scowling American military officer. Suddenly self-conscious in my uniform, I quickly glanced around to see if the other tourists—the Mexican tourists—were staring at me. I wondered what effect this image was having on them. Five million people—many of them Mexican school groups—visit Chapultepec Castle and experience this mural every year.

HANOI.

Driving or walking in Hanoi was unlike doing so anywhere else we'd ever been. There are eight million people living in Vietnam's capital, and by most estimates there are five million motorbikes. They swarm in packs of several hundred and flow in a way that must make sense to them but is incomprehensible to an outsider. Our escort had advised us that, when crossing a road, we should just keep moving. "The swarm will adjust to you," she said. Thankfully, she was right.

I was the first Chairman of the Joint Chiefs of Staff to visit Vietnam since Admiral Thomas Moorer went there near the end of the Vietnam War. The Vietnamese were eager to reestablish a relationship with us after forty years—especially because the Chinese were becoming very aggressive with them at sea and on their northern border.

We landed in Hanoi in the middle of a monsoon. *That monsoon scene in* Forrest Gump *was no exaggeration,* I thought to myself. We were greeted warmly by a large delegation who had braved the rain to meet us. The first official event would be an arrival ceremony—a parade in my honor—at the Vietnamese army headquarters the next day.

As we departed the hotel in the morning, the escort and translator who had been assigned to me got into the car, speaking rapidly on his phone in Vietnamese. Then he turned to me.

"We're a little early, General," he said. "The protocol officer at Vietnamese army headquarters recommends that we take a bit of a detour so we don't get there before they are ready for us."

"No problem," I replied. "I'd like to see some of the city before we begin our meetings."

Soon we were moving along unimaginably crowded city streets with swarms of motorbikes maneuvering around us. After just a few blocks, we turned off a main street onto a much less crowded one, and I noticed that we had picked up a police escort. We were traveling at a brisk thirty miles an hour or so, when suddenly we slowed to about ten. I glanced at the road ahead. There was no apparent reason for our reduced speed.

In the next moment, my translator directed my attention out the left window.

"General, on your left is the Vietnam Military History Museum."

In front of a large, long building in the French architectural style were rows of American military equipment: personnel carriers, tanks, artillery pieces, airplanes, and helicopters.

In my forty years of service, I had, of course, visited countless American military museums with displays of equipment captured from our enemies across the centuries and around the globe. But this was my first experience seeing our equipment displayed in someone else's museum. It was surreal.

The meetings went well. My counterpart and I discussed where we each were when our two countries were at war. I expressed appreciation for Vietnam's assistance in returning the remains of our missing-in-action. He expressed appreciation for our assistance in the ongoing efforts to mitigate the lingering effects of Agent Orange. We pledged to open a line of communication and to seek ways to increase our cooperation in Southeast Asia.

There was no mention made of my "side trip" past the museum. There didn't need to be.

GOOD GRIEF CAMP.

My aide handed me the schedule for the remainder of the day as I left the secretary of the Army's morning meeting. It was just my second month as chief of staff of the Army, and I was still adjusting to the pace of the job.

"What's this entry later this morning about visiting something called a Good Grief Camp?" I asked.

"I'm told that it's an annual gathering on Memorial Day weekend of spouses and children of the fallen, sir. It's held just a few miles away in Crystal City at the Marriott, and it's sponsored by an organization called the Tragedy Assistance Program for Survivors, 'TAPS' for short. They'd like you to be present for the opening ceremony and then meet with some children for a few minutes before you depart."

"Do you know how many children will be present?"

"No, sir. But I do know that each child is paired with a service member from the local area who volunteers to be their mentor for the weekend."

"Wow. That's impressive," I said. "Surprised I haven't heard of this before."

A couple of hours later, it was time to go to the Good Grief Camp. When I arrived, I learned that TAPS had taken over the entire Crystal City Marriott. Surviving family members were everywhere, moving from event to event. All of them—adults and children—wore bright-red polo shirts. I was introduced to Bonnie Carroll, who founded TAPS when she lost her husband in an aircraft accident in 1992.

"Bonnie, what are those buttons each of the family members is wearing?" I asked.

"Those are pictures of their lost loved ones," she said, more than a hint of emotion in her voice. I asked if I could see the button she wore in honor of her husband. She proudly told me his story.

"How many of you are here at the camp?" I asked.

"It increases every year as more and more survivors learn about it. This year we have four hundred adults and nearly five hundred children. The youngest child is four years old and the oldest is fourteen."

I stopped short.

"Five hundred children, each with a mentor? That's incredible. And the blue shirts?"

"Those are the mentors," she explained. "We have great participation from each of the services. We couldn't do it without them."

The opening ceremony was impressive and emotional. As it ended, Bonnie rejoined me to escort me to the large ballroom where the children were waiting.

"Any final thoughts about what you'd like me to say to the kids?" I asked.

"They can't wait to meet you," she said. "I'm sure they'll just want to ask you a few questions."

We were at the door. Someone pulled it open, and I walked in. The sight was truly overwhelming. Five hundred red-shirted children sitting cross-legged on the floor of this enormous ballroom; five hundred blue-shirted mentors sitting cross-legged at their sides. They had left a path clear for me to reach the center of the room. As I made my way through the crowd, I glanced around at the young faces and at the buttons they wore. Someone handed me a wireless microphone.

They're so joyful, I thought. *There must be something magical about bringing together these youngsters who share the experience of unimaginable grief.* I hoped I could honor them the way they deserved.

After giving a short explanation of who I was and why I was there, I asked if anyone had a question for me. Several dozen hands shot up. I pointed to a young man who looked to be about ten years old.

"What's your favorite pizza?" he asked.

"Pepperoni," I replied. "What's yours?"

"That's mine too," he replied happily. There was laughter and murmured affirmation that pepperoni was the way to go.

Next I pointed to a young teenage girl.

"Do you have your own airplane?" she asked.

"I do," I said. "I'm very lucky because I have to travel on it a lot."

There was a chorus of *oohs* and *ahhs* as the thought of a private airplane circulated through the room.

The questions and answers went on for about ten minutes. They were a lively bunch, and I shared my thoughts with them about school, sports, video games, popular music, and all the other things that children like to talk about. Eventually someone behind me announced that I had time for one more question. Sitting along the path I had walked on my way across the ballroom was a very young girl waving her hand enthusiastically. She was so cute. I walked over to her.

"What's your name?" I asked.

"Lizzy," she said confidently.

"How old are you, Lizzy?"

"I'm four years old," she replied.

"Well, what's your question, Lizzy?"

"Is my daddy an angel?"

Time stopped. The room got quiet. I could feel myself choking up.

"Of course your daddy is an angel, Lizzy," I said in a voice that was suddenly weaker than I needed it to be, hoping that no one would notice the tears welling in my eyes. "In fact, all of your mommies and daddies and brothers and sisters, and everyone on those buttons you're wearing, are angels. And it's because of them that we can all live the way we do. We love them."

The mood was somber now, and I knew I needed to recover. Maybe a song, something to leave them as happy as I had found them.

"Has anyone ever heard of a unicorn?" I asked, and broke into an Irish song about unicorns. It included hand motions to accompany the chorus. The kids were on their feet now, happily singing and gesturing along. At the end of the song, I thanked them and encouraged them to enjoy each other's company the rest of the weekend. They applauded and cheered. I suddenly felt somehow smaller than I had when I first met them.

As I returned to work, I knew that my brief time with those children would affect much more than the rest of my day.

Bonnie Carroll and Lizzy Yaggy remain part of my life to this day.

THE THANKSGIVING SECRET.

The two Secret Service agents were pretty blunt. "General, if word leaks out about this, we'll cancel the trip. It's that simple," the senior agent told me. I was in my office in an old avionics-repair facility at Baghdad Airport. Seven months earlier, the 1st Armored Division headquarters had taken up residence in one of the few airport administration buildings that had escaped destruction.

"Okay," I replied. "We'll make it happen."

The story of President Bush secretly flying from his Crawford, Texas, ranch to Baghdad to have Thanksgiving dinner with the troops in 2003 is pretty well known. At the direction of the Secret Service and the White House advance team, we had arranged for several hundred soldiers to be assembled just after sunset in a large dining tent in the middle of Baghdad Airport. We needed some plausible story to get them there, so we told them that the senior civilian official in Iraq, Jerry Bremer, wanted to talk with them and that a special entertainer would be appearing after dinner.

Soldiers are suspicious, and I heard them voice some of their suspicions as they entered the dining facility.

"I'll bet it's going to be Garth Brooks," said one.

"No, I'm thinking it's not an entertainer at all. It's probably the vice president," said another.

"Well, he's no entertainer. Besides, there's no way a politician is going to take the risk of flying into Baghdad right now," chimed in a third.

"You're probably right. Maybe it will be Britney Spears," a fourth soldier said hopefully.

When a little more than an hour later President Bush walked from behind a curtain and took his place on a small makeshift stage at the front of the tent, a collective roar went up from the crowd—a roar like I have never heard before or since. It was so loud that I feared our enemies might hear it, though they were probably ten or more miles away.

The applause and accompanying shouts went on for several minutes. I stood beside Condoleezza Rice, the national security adviser at the time, as tears streamed down both our faces. The president simply stood there, acknowledging the men and women before him and clearly moved by the experience.

There was something magical about that surprise visit. A commander in chief sharing with his soldiers a little of the danger that is a combat zone. No big policy statement, just a visible manifestation that what he was asking them to do was important. No fiery speech, just an unmistakable sense that he would support them and their families through this trial. No staged photographs, but he didn't decline a single soldier's request for a picture with him. It was much less what he said to them and much more how he interacted with them. He genuinely cared for them, and they knew it.

Walking out with President Bush to his waiting armored SUV for the short drive back to Air Force One, I thanked him for his visit and for his resolve. He stopped walking and turned to look at me.

"Don't you worry about my resolve," he said. "You just keep these young men and women focused and let me know what they need to get the job done. Our nation is blessed to have them, and," he added, "I'm blessed to be their commander in chief."

"Yes, sir," I replied. I saluted him as he stepped up into the SUV. The heavy door was closed, and he drove away.

It's not often that we are privileged to see into the heart of the commander in chief.

ONE DAY ON A PARADE FIELD.

It was a cold, gray February day at Fort Myer, Virginia, as I arrived at Conmy Hall. Arrayed before me were the U.S. Army Band and the combined ceremonial units of the Army, Navy, Air Force, and Marines. We were there to honor Leon Panetta, who was retiring after two years as secretary of defense. President Obama, Secretary Panetta, and I were seated on the dais. As we took our seats, a velvet-voiced narrator read Secretary Panetta's long list of accomplishments as secretary of defense. The son of Italian immigrants, he had amassed a long career of distinguished public service as a congressman, White House chief of staff, director of the CIA, and secretary of defense. Now he was being escorted across the parade field to review the troops one last time.

As I watched him walk across the field, I took in the crisp notes of the Army Band and the impressive spectacle of the servicemen and servicewomen standing before us in their impeccably groomed parade uniforms. *Secretary Panetta deserves this recognition*, I thought to myself.

I suddenly became aware that the president was leaning over to get my attention.

"Can you believe the three of us are here, Marty?" he whispered. Then he turned back to the parade field.

It took me a moment to realize what he was saying, to appreciate that the president of the United States was reflecting on the fact that the lives of an African American, an Italian American, and an Irish American had somehow managed to intersect at the highest level in the service of our country.

"Only in America, sir," I replied. He just nodded.

It's not often that we are privileged to see into the heart of the president of the United States.

Another former secretary of defense used to tell a story from his days as an undergraduate at Harvard. Each Sunday was movie night in his dormitory, and each movie night one of his more cynical classmates would wait for a dramatic moment in the movie and yell loudly and disruptively, "What does it mean?!"

That may not be the best behavior during movie night, but in thinking about memorable moments, it's the right question.

What does it mean? The answer is never "nothing."

CHAPTER SEVEN

SWEAT THE SMALL STUFF

MINUTE PARTICULARS
WEST POINT, 1970

"Mr. Dempsey," barked the senior cadet standing before me, clearly intending to be heard by the other thirty cadets standing in formation with me. "Did you shine your shoes with a Hershey bar today?"

"No, sir," I replied softly, clearly intending to minimize my embarrassment.

"What's that, Mr. Dempsey? I can't seem to hear you." He was practically shouting, even though his face was only inches from my own.

"No, sir," I replied more loudly.

"Then how do you explain the pitiful condition of your shoes?"

"No excuse, sir," I said, hoping to end the conversation.

"That's right, Mr. Dempsey. There is no excuse for your lack of attention to detail. I expect you to give your shoes a proper shine this evening and then bring them around to my room for reinspection."

"Yes, sir," I said as he finally moved on to the next plebe in line.

When you're a plebe at West Point, there's no detail too small to catch the attention of cadets who are senior to you. The very next day my belt buckle was inadequately shined and not aligned properly with the buttons on my shirt. The day after that it was the way I performed rifle manual, moving my ten-pound M14 rifle from the ground to my shoulder and back again. And then it was my failure to know how many lights there were in Cullum Hall, a historic building overlooking the parade field. *Why all this nitpicking?* I wondered. Surely these minutiae weren't worth so much trouble.

But in English class one day, I grudgingly began to understand this idea of attention to detail. The professor asked us to explain the meaning of a line from a poem by William Blake: "He who would do good to another must do it in ***minute particulars***." Typical college freshmen, we offered explanations that were all over the map, until one of my brighter classmates suggested that the poet was criticizing grand proclamations and grandiose promises about the "general good" and arguing that doing good and making real progress almost always starts small.

Sweat the small stuff, I thought to myself. *Maybe this relentless emphasis on attention to detail now is intended to develop habits that will help us solve the bigger problems that will come our way later.*

This epiphany would echo with me in the future, but it didn't help me on the way back from class that day, when a senior cadet stopped me because the brass plate on my hat wasn't shined to his satisfaction.

THE RULES OF GRAMMAR
WEST POINT, 1984

Master's degree in hand, I reported to West Point's English department in June 1984 and learned that I would be teaching four fifteen-cadet classes, two each day, in the upcoming fall semester. The subject was English composition, and all of my classes were scheduled for the afternoon. I immediately realized what that meant: not only would I have to teach these cadets how to write, but I would also have to figure out how to keep them awake after lunch. Recalling my own experiences as a cadet ten years earlier, I knew this would be no small task.

The course was designed to teach the young cadets how to write by making them write. Often. They wrote in class, and they wrote for homework. It was effective, but it sure made my life "sporty," teaching by day and grading papers by night.

Before they came to the Academy, most of these cadets had ranked near the top of their high school classes. They were poised and confident. Every once in a while, I'd come across one who was a little *too* confident.

Late one evening, grading papers at home, I came across one that was perplexing. It was clear from the introductory paragraph that the cadet had thought a lot about the topic, and he had crafted a solid thesis. However, reading further, I found his spelling and grammar almost impenetrable. I read and reread the paper, struggling to figure out what he was trying to accomplish, but it was as though he had invented his own language. I decided not to grade it and instead to have him visit me in my office the next day after class.

At the appointed time, he knocked on my half-open door.

"Cadet Murphy reporting as ordered, sir," he said, using the formal greeting required of all plebes.

"Good afternoon, Mr. Murphy. Have a seat."

"Thank you, sir." He took a seat on the other side of my desk.

"I want to talk with you about this paper," I said, retrieving it from a stack on my desk.

"That's what I figured, sir. I think I really nailed that one. Hope you agree," he said enthusiastically.

"Well, I don't, actually. The ultimate test of good writing is that it is persuasive, and I'm not persuaded by this paper. In fact, I'm not exactly sure what you were trying to accomplish with it. So I decided to give you a chance to explain before I assign a grade to it."

His demeanor suddenly became more serious. A cadet's academic performance can mean the difference between some relative freedom on the weekends and none at all.

"I'm not sure I understand, sir."

"Let me put it this way. I've never seen so many misspellings, so many sentence fragments, and such careless use of punctuation marks, especially the semicolon. I've also never seen some of the words you used. What were you trying to do?"

He smiled. Not exactly the response I had expected.

"Now I get it, sir," he said earnestly. "I probably should have told you, but I was writing in the style of William Faulkner. I had a similar assignment last year in a creative writing course at my high school, and my teacher really liked it."

He did not *just say that,* I thought.

"Listen, Mr. Murphy," I began. "I wouldn't think of stifling your creativity. But understand that you're in a basic composition course. The purpose of the course is to demonstrate your ability to think and write using the accepted signposts and traffic signals of the English language—the rules of grammar." I paused. "It would be helpful if you demonstrated that you can spell, too."

He was beginning to understand.

"Roger, sir," he said. "No more Faulkner."

"You're still missing the larger point here, Mr. Murphy. Faulkner didn't write like the Faulkner we know today the first time he picked up a pen. Only after he had mastered the rules of grammar did he begin twisting and turning them to create a particular effect. You haven't demonstrated that you understand the rules. Until you do, you can't violate them."

"I understand, sir."

"***Master the fundamentals first***," I told him. "Practice them often, and stray from them only if you understand the risk."

"Got it, sir." I could tell I had adequately made the point.

"I'll make a deal with you, Mr. Murphy," I said. "I'm going to give you a chance to rewrite this paper. If I were to grade it now, it would be a failing grade. I want you to return it to me in two days."

"Thank you, sir."

"Don't thank me yet. You've got a lot of work to do, and I'm not convinced you're as well grounded in the rules as you think you are. I'll see you in class in two days."

Popularized by John Adair's nine-dot puzzle in 1969, the phrase "thinking outside the box" became especially popular in the 1990s and early in the new century as shorthand for creative thinking. For a time, thinking outside the box was considered more important than understanding why "the box" worked in the first place. That's still sometimes the case, and it can be a problem.

I used to remind everyone, from commanders in combat to the Joint Chiefs, that "the box" got to be "the box" because it worked. That's not to say that there isn't a way to do things differently and better, only that we must understand the fundamentals, the basics, the small procedural details, before we decide to chart our own path.

Actually, *sweating the small stuff* is always the right place to start, whether we're writing an essay for English class or designing a military campaign.

PERFECT PRACTICE
FRIEDBERG, GERMANY, 1992

The short, muscular figure filling my doorway was my new command sergeant major, Don Stockton.

"Sir, do you have a minute?" he asked.

"Of course, Sergeant Major," I replied.

I had been in command of the 4th Battalion, 67th Armor Regiment—known as "the Bandits"—for a year. It was a storied unit with a distinguished history dating back to World War II. Under my command were fifty-eight M1A1 tanks, manned and supported by forty officers and five hundred enlisted soldiers.

"Thanks, sir," he said as he took a seat at a small table. I joined him there.

"What's on your mind, Sergeant Major?"

I had known Don Stockton for only a few weeks. He had replaced a command sergeant major who had been with the battalion for almost seven years. That first command sergeant major had become far too set in his ways, and it had been a difficult year for me working with him. Don Stockton was young, smart, and fit. I was very excited when he joined the battalion.

The command sergeant major is the senior enlisted soldier in the battalion. The position has no direct authority—by law only officers can command—but has enormous influence on the battalion's day-to-day activities. Commanders rely on their command sergeant major for advice on all matters related to the enlisted ranks. When you get one like Don Stockton, you can rely on him or her for advice about practically anything.

"Sir, I'd like your permission to change the way we're approaching physical readiness training," he began. "Have you ever heard the Vince Lombardi quote about practice?" I shook my head. "Well, Lombardi said that it's not practice that makes perfect; it's perfect practice that makes perfect."

"I like that," I replied. "Makes sense, especially in our line of work. I take it you've seen some areas in our training where we're not reinforcing that idea. What do you have in mind?"

"Well, for starters, I want to get the junior sergeants involved. Right now they're along for the ride. They don't take ownership. Hell, I'm not even sure they know how to plan good physical training, let alone execute it." He was warming to his topic now, speaking with great enthusiasm. "More important, as we give them responsibility, I want to hold them accountable not just for the execution of physical training but also for the *perfect* execution of physical training."

"Go on," I said.

"Here's the deal, sir. We need everything we do to reflect how we'll fight." He pointed out that we usually fought in small teams (sections of two or platoons of four tanks), occasionally in larger teams (companies of fourteen tanks), and sometimes were given a mission that required maneuvering the entire battalion.

I told him I agreed, then asked what he was proposing.

"We make our physical readiness training consistent with the reality of how we fight," he answered. "Most of the time we should do our physical training in small teams. On occasion we should do it in larger teams. And sometimes we should do it as a battalion. We should make our movements and our commands consistent with our doctrine. For example, when we do a battalion run every two weeks or so, we put the scouts out front, you receive reports along the route of march, we react to ambushes and breach obstacles, we plan to refuel with water stops along the way. Physical readiness training becomes a way to empower our junior leaders, a way to reinforce how we fight, and a way to reemphasize that only perfect practice makes perfect."

I was impressed and told him so. "How long do you think it will take you to implement?" I asked.

"I can have the adjustment made to our physical readiness training in less than a month. But this one change won't matter unless we can get our young men and women to accept that only perfect practice can make perfect in all of our activities. In maintenance, in rifle marksmanship, in tank gunnery, in field exercises, in everything we do."

We began implementing his changes right away.

It's hard to overstate the change that Command Sergeant Major Stockton made in the way the Bandits trained in the year we were together. He was tireless and relentless. He was a patient coach and stern taskmaster. His admonition about perfect practice became part of our vocabulary. Before him, we had been doing well in a lot of areas; with him we did well in everything we touched. It all started with a commitment to master the details, the small stuff, the things that are the preconditions of perfection.

My time in the Bandits with Command Sergeant Major Stockton helped me understand that perfection is almost always elusive but always worth the effort. It helped me understand that an important step in accomplishing any task is to first *sweat the small stuff.*

REKINDLING THE FUNDAMENTALS
BAGHDAD, 2003

In August 2003, on a base camp in Baghdad, one of my soldiers was wounded by a negligent discharge. A negligent discharge occurs when a soldier improperly clears their weapon after returning to base camp from a mission and the weapon goes off. Fortunately, the soldier survived, but he had to be medically evacuated. Although this was the first casualty, it was the third negligent discharge since I had taken command the previous month.

In August 2003, a tank crew inadvertently discharged the fire-suppression system on their tank. No one was injured, but the tank was rendered inoperable for several weeks. In one battalion, four of forty-four tanks experienced power-plant failures due to a problem with the air-induction system—in layman's terms, the tank engines failed because the crew failed to properly clean the air filters. Another battalion administered a tank gunnery skills test—an assessment of basic skills related to the safe operation of the tank—with a 25 percent failure rate.

In August 2003, the division experienced six heat casualties, including one fatality. This was in spite of policies we had in place to limit heat exposure, reduce workloads, and monitor those most susceptible to heat injury.

In August 2003, a battalion commander administered a physical fitness test to her soldiers that resulted in a 30 percent failure rate.

These statistics were presented to me at a monthly review and analysis session with my staff. I called a meeting with the six senior colonels commanding my six brigades to get their insights into what was happening. All agreed the trends were worrisome. Most agreed they indicated a lack of discipline. However, there was considerable disagreement on how to deal with it.

"Sir, we can't overreact to these trends," said one brigade commander. "We're in a combat zone, after all."

"Yes, we are," said another, "but these statistics make it clear that we're developing some bad habits. I know we don't want to do anything to distract us from the mission, but shouldn't overcoming these failures be part of our mission too?"

These comments began a spirited discussion among the most senior commanders and their command sergeants major about the relative seriousness of the failures and what to do about them. I was pleased. As with most issues, I knew we would find both challenges and opportunities in this one.

After allowing the discussion to go on for a while, I added my own insights.

"Let me assure you that I know everyone is working as hard as they can possibly work in this incredibly complex environment. The question is whether we're staying true to what got us here."

"What do you mean, sir?" one of the brigade commanders asked.

"Well, most of you got here in April. I joined you here in June. I wasn't with you during your preparation and the first part of your mission, but I know you were a well-trained, disciplined unit. My question is whether that's still true. We have to confront the possibility that we've become so focused on daily combat operations that we're losing our focus on the fundamentals. If we are, we need to figure out what we should do about it."

I had a very talented group of brigade commanders. They acknowledged that even though we were 32,000 strong, they were having trouble meeting the competing requirements of patrol schedules, key-leader engagements with Iraqi officials, and the protection of critical infrastructure in this sprawling city of seven million people. They agreed that the fundamentals were beginning to fray, and they wanted to help figure out how to reverse the trend.

I thanked them and promised we'd come up with a plan within the next week.

Two days later we were told we wouldn't be going home before Christmas. I had considered it only a remote possibility anyway, but the news that we'd be in Iraq for a full year, through the following April, was disheartening, especially to our many married soldiers.

The next day I asked my two superb assistant division commanders, Mark Hertling and Mike Scaparrotti, to join me for breakfast to discuss how to link both the erosion of fundamentals and the extended stay in Iraq into something positive. If anybody could figure this out, I knew it would be these two. They were both hard-nosed, combat-tested operators and compassionate leaders.

Mike was the assistant division commander for operations. He spoke first.

"On the training side, I think we can construct rifle ranges on each of our big bases. I'm also told that there's an old Iraqi gunnery range about thirty miles east of Baghdad, near a village called Besmaya, that we might be able to use for our tanks and infantry fighting vehicles. I'll have the staff put together training guidance and a schedule that requires everyone to qualify with their individual weapon and their combat vehicle as soon as we can cycle them through. That should get at many of the problems we've been having with our weapons systems."

Mark was the assistant division commander for logistics. He spoke next.

"Now that we know we're here for another eight months, we need to get really serious about doing periodic services on our vehicles. I'll make sure we have the necessary service kits, and the brigades can begin scheduling services. I also suggest that we have each unit initiate or—for those that already have them—jump-start a driver training program. We've changed out some drivers, and we've also received additional vehicles. Refocusing on proper driving and maintaining in this environment will help a lot."

This all sounded good, but it would also create additional tasks for a group of junior leaders who already felt overstretched. We needed something to balance it out—and to offset the blow to morale from what many soldiers saw as their deployment being extended by five months.

"Is there anything we can do locally to get soldiers off the line for a few days and let them clear their minds for a while?" I asked. The Army had not yet initiated a "rest and relaxation" (R&R) leave policy. That wouldn't come for a few more months.

"I've actually been looking around for someplace where we could do that," Mark replied immediately. "There's an abandoned Republican

Guard officers' club inside the Green Zone with several dozen rooms, a conference facility, a kitchen, and a pool. It suffered some bomb damage early in the war, but I think our engineers can repair it. I'll start asking around about how we could take control of it."

That sounded perfect.

Not surprisingly, given the talent we had at every level of the division, it all came together pretty quickly. The soldiers were actually eager to refresh their marksmanship skills on the rifle ranges inside their base camps. The gunnery range we built at Besmaya became hard to schedule, because everyone in the division wanted to use it. Vehicle services and driver training became part of our daily routine again. The R&R facility we reconstructed inside the Green Zone—christened "Freedom Rest"—was always filled to capacity as commanders took advantage of the opportunity to give their soldiers a much-needed break.

And, not surprisingly, all of the negative trend lines related to safety, discipline, training, and maintenance began to improve.

The vast majority of books and articles about warfare focus on the big, violent, decisive battles. As it turns out, big battles occur infrequently, especially in the kind of warfare we waged in Iraq. So keeping our edge—our advantages in training and discipline—becomes the biggest challenge. And that challenge requires a focus on the fundamentals.

We've all heard people in all walks of life tell us, "Don't sweat the small stuff." My experiences suggest otherwise: that it's always important to *sweat the small stuff.* Provided you've correctly identified the most important fundamentals for your organization, the "small stuff" will guide you through even the toughest challenges.

THE CHAIRMAN'S THREE RULES
THE PENTAGON, 2012

Shortly after I became chairman, I walked into the Situation Room for my first meeting of the Principals Committee. Seated at the head of the table was Tom Donilon, the national security adviser. Several seats away, across from where I saw my nameplate positioned, was our ambassador to the UN, Susan Rice. I had known her for fifteen years, since she was an assistant secretary of state for Africa and I was a colonel in the Directorate of Plans and Policy on the Joint Staff. She was studying her briefing material but looked up and saw me.

"Hello, Marty. It's great to have you on the team," she said.

"Thanks, Ambassador. I'm not sure it's sunk in yet, but I hope I can contribute to the team. There's plenty going on in the world."

"What's with this 'Ambassador' stuff?" she asked. "We go back a long way."

Before I could answer, Mr. Donilon called the meeting to order.

After the meeting, Ambassador Rice approached me.

"Seriously, Marty," she said. "Please call me 'Susan.' We're going to be spending a lot of time together in this room."

"That's precisely why I need to call you 'Ambassador,'" I explained. "First of all, you've earned the title. But more important, there will be times in this room when we don't agree with each other. In those times, I don't want there to be hard feelings or any awkwardness about relationships I may have had with each of you at other times and in other places. I trust you understand."

"Okay, *General*, have it your way." She smiled as she walked away.

There were similar exchanges with the other principals early in my time as chairman. I always addressed them as "Secretary" or "Director" or "Chief" or "Ambassador," as appropriate. Most of the time they called me "Chairman" or "General."

It felt right, and this was one small thing I did to ensure I held up my side of the civilian-military relationship while I was chairman.

When I became chairman, the White House and the military had just gone through a difficult period. The military thought the White House was micromanaging it. The White House thought the military was withholding reasonable options for force levels in Afghanistan. In fact, each had reason to believe as it did. Our system is designed to generate creative friction within the executive branch and among the three branches of government. It works, provided the friction remains creative.

There were other ways in which I reminded myself about the importance of relationships in keeping things creative—mostly small habits, including three that I eventually articulated to my staff and schedulers as "The Chairman's Three Rules":

Accept no awards while chairman. The myriad organizations around the country that support our military, our wounded, our veterans, and their families often invite the chairman to receive awards. These are always well intended and usually presented to the chairman "on behalf of the men and women of the armed forces." However, it never felt right to me to be feted and honored in ballrooms while a quarter million men and women in uniform were deployed across the globe at any given time. Sometimes, when I could, I would agree to go and talk to these groups about the remarkable service of our soldiers, sailors, airmen, and marines. But I declined domestic awards for the entirety of my time as chairman and did the same for foreign awards until the last six months of my tour of duty. It helped remind me that service is its own reward.

Decline personal-profile media pieces while chairman. Chairmen of the Joint Chiefs of Staff cannot escape the interest of the media. Nor should they. If America's parents are going to share their sons and daughters with the military, they have a right to hear from the most senior military leaders about why the national security issues of the day are important. So the chairman is often invited to appear on television shows, radio shows, and podcasts to explain how strategy and policy contribute to national security. However, in my judgment, the chairman shouldn't compete with our elected and appointed civilian leaders as a media personality. Therefore, I routinely declined requests for personal-profile and human-interest stories about me or my family. I tried to keep the media attention I received focused on the Joint Force.

Avoid appearances on late-night comedy shows while chairman. These are some of the most popular shows on television and connect with large and diverse groups of people across the country. Moreover, they are willing to allow senior military leaders to appear in uniform to help them get their message out. However, they are comedy shows, often with a political edge, and I never felt comfortable trying to reconcile that with the deadly serious business of military service and the importance of remaining apolitical. Declining such appearances felt like the consistent thing to do.

These small habits can seem trivial in the scope of responsibilities of the Chairman of the Joint Chiefs of Staff. Yet relationships often improve or decay based on just such small, seemingly trivial issues. As in any other endeavor, I found it important as chairman to sweat the small stuff as a habit before tackling the larger complexities of national security.

It's always important to identify the fundamentals—the small stuff—on which an organization is built. Most failures can be traced back to an erosion of the fundamentals. It's understandable that people in an organization often conclude that they are under-resourced and too busy. That's human nature. But when we use that to ignore the fundamentals, to cut corners, we end up paying a price.

Sweat the small stuff, and you'll have a much better chance of getting the big stuff right.

CHAPTER EIGHT

EXERCISE SENSIBLE SKEPTICISM

A LIBERAL EDUCATION
WEST POINT, 1971

When cadets get an opportunity to leave West Point on a trip with an athletic team or academic club, or on a weekend pass, it's best not to get in their way. Time away from the regimented Academy life is prized, and every second counts. Through the years, but especially since the U.S. military became an all-volunteer force, cadets have usually been warmly welcomed wherever they travel. They are not hard to pick out of a crowd, and the youngest among them often travel in uniform—granted the privilege of having civilian clothes only as upperclassmen.

However, there have been times in the Academy's more than two hundred years when our military has not been held in the same esteem it is today, times when leaving West Point could bring edgy, heated questions, disapproving looks, and even verbal slurs. The summer of 1971 was one of those times.

On March 16, 1968, in the Vietnamese hamlet of My Lai, American soldiers massacred between four hundred and five hundred unarmed civilians, mostly women and children. When the incident was discovered in November 1969, it quickly and severely eroded support for U.S. involvement in the Vietnam War. Though twenty-six soldiers were charged with criminal offenses, only one, Lieutenant William Calley Jr., was convicted. His trial took place between November 1970 and March 1971, and its details sparked widespread outrage.

That summer, right after I had completed my plebe year and arrived home to stay for a month, I was called a "baby killer" for the first time. And not by some stranger. By a grammar-school classmate I had known most of my life. Not everyone in my hometown was so outspoken, but there was an unmistakable awkwardness in the many conversations I had with friends and relatives about the war that summer.

The Vietnam War was a searing experience for those drafted to fight there, and it was polarizing at home. Lined up against opponents of the war were those who subscribed to the idea of "my country, right or wrong." Just as the "baby killer" moniker didn't sit well with me, neither did the idea that anything done in the name of the country must be right.

It was a confusing time when peace signs and jingoistic slogans competed on bumper stickers across America.

There was a certain comfort in returning to West Point after a month at home—not because I was back among those who universally supported the war, but quite the opposite: I was back among those who believed the Vietnam War would soon be theirs to wage and wanted earnestly to understand it. I was back among classmates and instructors who encouraged me to challenge both the idea that the war was a lost cause and the notion that it should not be questioned simply because it was the policy of the U.S. government. I was back in an institution that provided and promoted a liberal education as essential in the preparation for becoming a military officer.

I didn't know it at the time, but those days were just the beginning of a journey in learning how to listen, to learn, to question, to argue, to communicate, to apply knowledge and skills to real-world problems honestly and with an open mind. Later, long after I had graduated from West Point, I would make sure those around me knew that I would always welcome, even expect, a bit of *sensible skepticism.*

A LESSON IN LATENCY
COMBAT MANEUVER TRAINING CENTER, GERMANY, 1992

There are three places in the Army where soldiers and leaders are tested in conditions that replicate combat conditions as closely as possible. One of them is in the hilly German countryside near Hohenfels, Germany. The terrain there is complex, compartmented, and heavily vegetated. There are fully functioning villages. Role players roam the countryside as civilians on the battlefield.

The enemy—euphemistically called the "opposing force" (OPFOR)—are U.S. soldiers just like us, but they are permanently stationed there, which means they know the nuances of the terrain, have seen a lot of training units come and go, and so have a decided home-field advantage. A typical training event lasts three weeks, with five or six battles waged in continuous operations over that time. It's not uncommon for the OPFOR to win five out of six. The point is to encourage us to learn, and we tend to learn more in failure than in success. Better there than on a real battlefield later on.

That's not to say we're not competitive. The battles can be very intense and often turn on a single decision. In that regard, it's very realistic.

I had been to Hohenfels before, but in the spring of 1992 I was taking my own tank battalion to the training area. This was my first trip as the commander, and I was eager to see how I could do in this challenging environment.

By the end of the first week, we were feeling pretty good about ourselves. We had held our own in each of the first three battles. I felt like we were jelling as a team. Next up was the toughest battle of all. We were given forty-eight hours to establish a deliberate defense. Few beat the OPFOR when they are massed and on the attack, so this was the one we really wanted to win.

The staff had prepared the operations order that would guide our actions and help me make decisions during the fight. The next step was to rehearse the plan around a terrain model, with the commanding general of the training center in attendance. The actual battle would follow the next morning.

There were three parallel north-south corridors on which the enemy could attack us. We couldn't be equally strong on all three, but neither could the enemy, so we wanted to mask our strength and position a reserve to react once the enemy made his intentions known. Typically, the enemy commander wouldn't decide where to place his main effort until he believed he knew how we were arrayed. It would be a game of cat and mouse, with each of us seeking exactly the right moment to strike.

For planning purposes, we numbered the corridors 1, 2, and 3. We were going to be strongest in corridor 2, solid in corridor 1, and by our perceived weakness encourage the enemy to attack along corridor 3, where our reserve was well positioned to interdict him. It was a simple plan—most successful plans are simple—and the rehearsal went well. We were ready.

In training rehearsals, we spend the most time on the key decisions that the commander will make during the fight—usually only two or three—and what information he or she will need in order to make them. Several times during this rehearsal, we stressed that the key piece of information we needed was when the enemy commander sent more than two of his companies—more than half his force—into corridor 3. We decided to place additional scouts in an advantageous position to make that call.

As I settled into my tank in the center sector, I felt good about how this battle would unfold, and I wasn't disappointed. The enemy perceived weakness in corridor 3, I received the report that he was pushing his main effort there, and I committed the reserve to meet it. Then I awaited word that our reserve had interdicted the enemy and that we had carried the day.

Except that the word I received was that the enemy had penetrated our rear area and destroyed all of our logistics. We had lost. I was stunned.

There would be an after-action review about an hour later where we would find out what had happened. Just a few minutes after the battle, though, the commanding general drove up to my tank in his HUMMWV. I dismounted to greet him.

"How are you, sir?" I asked.

Brigadier General Montgomery Meigs was well known to all of us. He was the great-great-great-grandnephew of General Montgomery Meigs, the quartermaster general of the Union Army during the Civil War. He was also a serious student of warfare.

"Hello, Colonel," he said. "What do you think just happened here?"

"I'm not sure, sir. The enemy did what I'd hoped he'd do. I had all of my forces arrayed where I wanted them. I had the information I needed. I made the call, but the enemy still managed to penetrate us. I'm frustrated."

"Well, don't be frustrated," he said. "But there is an important lesson to be learned here."

"What's that, sir?"

"The lesson of is—was—gonna be."

"Is—was—gonna be? Can't say that's something I've studied in our doctrine."

"I know. And that's a problem. I've seen a lot of very talented commanders pass through here and make the same mistake you just made."

"What mistake is that?"

"You're dealing with the information you receive as though you're receiving it in real time."

I was puzzled. "What do you mean, sir?"

"Well, think about it," he said. "When you receive a report from your scouts or from one of your subordinate commanders, you're thinking about it as though it *is*—that is, as though you're receiving the report in real time. But by the time you receive it, it's actually *was*. That is, it's past tense. And what you really need in order to make decisions is a feeling for what's *gonna be*. You want to know where the enemy will be when you make your decision."

I still didn't understand how that insight applied to our failure in the rehearsal.

He explained: "When you received the report about where the enemy was focusing their main effort, you thought about it as though you were receiving it in real time. But some period of time elapsed between when your scouts saw the enemy acting and when the report made its way to you. I don't think you accounted for the latency between the enemy's action, your scout's reaction, and your receipt of the report."

"Probably not, sir," I conceded.

"So you thought you were making the right decisions at the right time, but you were shooting behind the target. How far behind the target you find yourself depends on how much confidence you have in your subordinates to report in a timely fashion."

"Thanks, sir. That's really helpful. Any advice on what I should do in the future?"

"Develop your instinct to interpret the information you receive. You need to compare the information you receive against your experiences and instincts, and then make a decision. Never take any information you receive on the battlefield at face value. We expect commanders to be **sensibly skeptical** about the information they receive, until they accept it based on their experience and instincts. Trust your instincts, and you'll make better decisions."

"Appreciate it, sir. I wish we had a do-over on this one. I'd like to apply the lesson of is–was–gonna be."

"We can arrange that," he said.

And he did. Several days later, we were put into a hasty defense with the same mission but on different terrain. Based on what I had learned, I positioned our scouts differently, interpreted their reports differently, and made my decisions differently. We pinned the enemy in a position where they couldn't maneuver and defeated them decisively. It felt good to succeed where just a few days earlier we had failed.

Because of technological advances, we might convince ourselves that our information-latency challenges are behind us. We might conclude that since information is ubiquitous and available to us all the time, everywhere, and on the move, we can gather what we need in the moment and make prudent, effective decisions in real time. But actually, information overload most often produces information paralysis. We convince ourselves that if only we had one more exquisite missing piece of information, we could make a better decision, and then the moment passes us by.

The lesson of is–was–gonna be is that experience, judgment, and instinct matter in decision making. Leaders are always at their best when they take the information available to them and apply a standard of **sensible skepticism** to it.

DROP A ZERO

IRAQ, 2006

Trying to rebuild the Iraqi army from 2005 to 2007 may be the most challenging job I ever had. It wasn't that they weren't well-meaning young men willing to serve their country under very challenging circumstances. They were. But they had an unfathomably romanticized memory of their capabilities. Stated more bluntly, they thought they and their predecessors in the Iraqi Republican Guard were much better soldiers than they actually were.

It was hard to overcome. I visited most of the seventy-five or so battalions we had organized, trained, housed, and equipped during those two years. The visits were surprisingly, and disappointingly, similar.

The Iraqi battalion in Ramadi, just west of Fallujah, was one of the best. It was also among those that had seen the most combat. I was eager to interact with the leadership of the battalion to learn how they were adapting to their very difficult mission.

My helicopter began its descent into the Ramadi battalion's base camp. As it touched down, I jumped out and strode over to meet the Iraqi battalion commander. We exchanged salutes.

"Good morning, Colonel," I said. "It's good to meet you."

"Greetings, General," he replied. "We are honored by your visit."

I had no idea how honored they were until I looked over his shoulder and saw an Iraqi soldier holding a goat on a tether in one hand and a dagger in the other. As the battalion commander directed my attention that way, the soldier slit the goat's throat. I knew I would see it later at lunch.

"I'm looking forward to getting your insights into how things are going in Ramadi and in Al Anbar Province," I told the battalion commander.

"I have a briefing prepared for you, Your Excellency."

We were ushered into his headquarters, where we were offered tea, Arabic coffee, and cookies. I was familiar with the tradition and knew enough to be respectful of it. After an appropriate amount of time, I suggested to the colonel that we move into the conference room for the briefing.

It began with the colonel's assessment of the enemy activity in his area. He explained that Al Qaeda was very active in Ramadi and that because many of his countrymen distrusted the Iraqi government, it was very difficult to root them out.

I acknowledged the challenge. Distrust of the Iraqi government was the common refrain among the country's Sunni population.

"How many of the enemy are you fighting here in Ramadi, Colonel?" I asked.

"Three thousand," he replied without hesitation.

"You have good sources to validate that number?"

"I do. We are facing three thousand Al Qaeda fighters," he answered with conviction.

Just a few days earlier, I had been briefed by the senior U.S. intelligence officer in Iraq, who stated with some confidence that the strength of Al Qaeda in *all* of Iraq was just over two thousand. I let it pass.

"And how many soldiers do you have in your battalion?" I asked.

"Almost one thousand," he replied.

Before I had flown out to Ramadi, the U.S. adviser to this battalion had reported that its strength had fallen to under seven hundred.

"So you've got enough soldiers to maintain security here in Ramadi?"

"*Hamdillilah*," he replied. Thanks be to God.

This wasn't an unusual exchange with Iraqi battalion commanders. They were quick to overestimate the challenges they were facing, for fear that they would be criticized for lack of progress. They were quick to overestimate the strength and readiness of their battalions, for fear that their payroll would be cut.

We had long ago decided that, when receiving Iraqi military leaders' assessments of the enemy's numbers, their own strength, or the size of crowds during demonstrations, we should "drop a zero." This was no exception.

Building the Iraqi army and police was an exercise in *sensible skepticism*. It was clear that decades of living under a harsh dictator had ingrained in their leaders a habit of exaggeration. Some exaggerated because they were clearly corrupt; most exaggerated because they were simply afraid. We worked hard to train, educate, and encourage Iraq's nascent military leaders, but we didn't manage to break that habit on my watch. Given the state of Iraqi politics, I doubt that it's been broken even today.

IN SEARCH OF A COMMON PICTURE
AFGHANISTAN, 2014

From time to time, the White House or the secretary of defense will ask for a review of our military operations around the world. Specifically, they do this when annual decisions approach about the defense share of the federal budget and about how to resource extended campaigns such as those in Iraq and Afghanistan. It's important that policy makers, intelligence professionals, and senior military leaders come to some agreement about whether progress is being made consistent with expectations.

If you've ever seen the 2008 movie *Vantage Point*, you'll have a pretty good idea of how difficult it is to get these different communities to agree upon a common picture. In the movie, eight strangers with eight different vantage points describe an assassination attempt on the president of the United States, complicating the work of authorities urgently trying to find the perpetrators.

The review of our mission in Afghanistan in 2014 was an important one. In December 2014, NATO and the United States formally ended their thirteen-year combat mission in Afghanistan, handing over responsibility for security to Afghan forces. Based on the 2014 review, the president was going to consider the first step in a series of troop withdrawals.

I was in my office in the Pentagon when the director of the Joint Staff, Air Force lieutenant general Dave Goldfein, asked to see me.

"Good morning, sir," he said.

"Hello, Fingers," I replied. In all our time together, I never did learn why his call sign was "Fingers," but Dave Goldfein was an outstanding officer with a distinguished combat record. He would eventually be selected as Chief of Staff of the Air Force.

"Sir," he said, "we've just received General Austin's campaign review of our mission in Afghanistan."

"Good. What do you think?"

"I think it's very well done, sir. But CENTCOM's assessment is significantly different from the intelligence community's assessment, which we've also just received in draft."

"Let me guess," I said. "The intelligence community's assessment is that Afghanistan is a lost cause, the Taliban are in ascendance, and the Afghan army is incapable of protecting anything."

"That's about right, sir."

"And CENTCOM's assessment is that we only need one more year and there will be significant improvement," I continued.

"Right again, sir. You sound a bit skeptical of both."

"Well, I think we should always be a bit skeptical, especially when such important decisions hang in the balance. Part of our problem is that the personalities behind these assessments, both in the intelligence community and in our mission in Afghanistan, change frequently. And institutionally there's a difference in how we each think about risk. When the intelligence community submits an assessment, they get an A or an F. That's it. No other grade. They're either right or they're wrong. That's rough. And as for the military, we don't think there's any problem we can't solve."

"I agree, sir. I've seen it time and time again. Well-meaning, intelligent people trying to do the right thing," Fingers offered.

"No question about that," I replied. "By the way, the president knows that, and he's generally fine with the differences, but eventually he has to make important decisions about the budget and the commitment of forces. He'd like a little help, and I'd like to give it to him. If the president makes a decision about Afghanistan based on incorrect or incomplete information, and we don't like it, we'll have no one to blame but ourselves." I paused for a moment to consider the challenge ahead.

"Here's what we need to do," I continued. "I know CENTCOM doesn't always appreciate us questioning their analysis, but please have our staff work with theirs to do a side-by-side comparison of the two assessments for me. I'd like to understand the differences and see where that takes us. I know the president will call for a National Security Council meeting soon to discuss the way ahead in Afghanistan, and I want to be ready."

The next day I received the side-by-side analysis, and there were indeed differences. The assessment of the intelligence community was generally more pessimistic about the future of the mission in Afghanistan than the military assessment. There were legitimate reasons for the differences. Some aspects of the mission were relatively easy to measure: the number of attacks, the number of trained Afghan soldiers, the number of districts under the control of the legitimate Afghan government. Others were more difficult: the willingness of Afghan political leaders to work together, the quality and loyalty of the leaders of the Afghan army, whether Taliban control of a district headquarters building indicated their control of the entire district. It's not unreasonable for two experts to look at the same data and reach different conclusions.

The director of the Joint Staff was back in my office.

"What do you think, sir?" he asked.

"Well, I don't think it's appropriate to ask either the intelligence community or CENTCOM to change their assessments just because they come to different conclusions. I assume they've spoken about the differences."

"They have, sir," Fingers replied. "In fact, the intelligence community has agreed to place a text box on the first page of their report in which they acknowledge CENTCOM's difference of opinion about the likelihood of our success in Afghanistan."

"That's good," I said. "The question I need to grapple with is how best to advise the president, so that he's not left to make an irreconcilable choice between two significantly different assessments."

Personal relationships matter all the time, but especially when big decisions are complicated by competing and sometimes conflicting information (which in my experience happens all the time). So I discussed the assessments in separate conversations with General Austin at CENTCOM and with the director of the CIA. I told General Austin that there were some parts of the military assessment in which I had more confidence—and therefore intended to be more assertive—and that, based on my own experience, I was *sensibly skeptical* about the other parts. I told the director of the CIA the same thing about the intelligence assessment. We all agreed to work together to pragmatically and unemotionally paint a picture for the president, so that he could eventually make the important decisions that only he could make. In the end, we made progress in reconciling our differences, though differences still remained.

The National Security Council meeting occurred a week or so later. The assessments were presented, the discussions were inclusive and professional, and the necessary decisions were made.

When I returned from the meeting, Fingers was waiting to hear how it had gone.

"It went well, actually," I told him.

"Great, sir. So we're in a good place with our mission and our projected force levels in Afghanistan for the next year?"

"Well, based on what we know today, we've made some pragmatic modifications to our objectives. I'm confident we have the guidance and the resources necessary to accomplish them as they've been modified. But, as we both know, Afghanistan is a very complex and dynamic problem. It's important that we continue to challenge our thinking about it."

Before we moved on to our next challenges, I decided it was important to back-brief the staff officers who had worked on this issue for the past two weeks, preparing the side-by-side comparison of the assessments and getting me ready for the NSC meeting. They had worked hard, and I knew they would appreciate the recognition and feedback.

Several days later, Fingers accompanied five young staff officers into my office. They took seats around the table.

"Ladies and gentlemen," I said to them, "I want to thank you for your hard work on this year's Afghanistan review. Do you have any questions about the process?"

One of them spoke up immediately. "Yes, sir. How did the NSC resolve the differences in our assessments about the prospects for a positive future for Afghanistan?" she asked.

"Great question," I responded. "Let me begin to answer it by saying that I've been reviewing assessments of Afghanistan since I commanded CENTCOM in 2008. What I've learned is that no one is apathetic about Afghanistan. It's an issue that generates strong feelings and deep conviction."

"We've sure seen that," another young officer put in.

"So in working out our differences," I continued, "we first agree that there's no sense getting angry with each other. It's the intelligence analysts' job to tell it like they see it, and it's our job to tell it like we see it. We're asked for separate assessments with the understanding that there will be some friction between them. My job, and the job of the other advisers to the president, is to make sure it's creative friction."

"That sounds right, sir, but how do you do that?"

"Well, we keep asking for more information, but eventually the shot clock runs out and we need to make a decision. At that point we count on our experience, judgment, and instincts. I think of it as applying a standard of *sensible skepticism* to all but the most verifiable information and then making a decision—in this case, a decision on what we will recommend to the president."

"That's helpful, sir. Thanks for letting us know," one of the young officers said. They all nodded in agreement.

"Thank you again for your hard work on these important issues. Now back to work!" I smiled as they stood and filed out.

"I appreciate you doing that, sir," Fingers said once they had departed.

"We're lucky to have them."

☆ ☆ ☆ ☆

Sensible skepticism means thinking hard about the information we receive, not just blithely accepting it. It means overcoming decision paralysis by reaching a point when you allow yourself to be satisfied with the information you have. It means managing relationships between leaders and followers in an open and transparent way.

Looking ahead, I think this will become even more important. The nexus of artificial intelligence (AI), quantum computing, and big-data management to manipulate information, corrupt databases, and produce things like deepfake images means that sensible skepticism may become more important than any of the hard skills we associate with decision making today. Increasingly, sensible skepticism will be a hedge against the likelihood that data may be manipulated in ways that we cannot even conceive of today.

CHAPTER NINE

BE RESPONSIBLY REBELLIOUS

CHILDREN OF THE SIXTIES
WEST POINT, 1970

It would be a stretch to suggest that I encountered a great deal of rebelliousness at West Point. The institution responsible for developing America's military leaders obviously doesn't set out to encourage rebelliousness. But it would also be a mistake—and a disservice to my clever and adventurous classmates—to suggest that rebelliousness was entirely absent.

We arrived at West Point in July 1970, just after the end of the turbulent sixties, which had brought dramatic changes in social norms affecting everything from clothing to music to drugs to sexuality. We came to West Point out of the tumult of the civil rights movement, student activism, large-scale Great Society programs, and a long, unpopular war.

As children of the sixties, we were used to questioning authority, comfortable with change, and fully capable of exhibiting a rebellious streak. That said, we were also smart enough—and had enough interest in graduating—to channel our inchoate rebelliousness well within the boundaries defined by West Point's rules and regulations.

For their part, the Academy's leaders were sufficiently attuned to the times to seek our input on important issues like potential changes in the treatment of plebes; the honor code; academic workloads; and modifications to summer training. An old joke at the time described West Point as "170 years of tradition unhampered by progress." It was more complicated than that.

We graduated four years later with a sense that change almost always starts with a bit of rebelliousness. Through the years, in a variety of walks of life, we would learn how to recognize when rebelliousness should be nurtured and when it should be neutered.

RETHINKING BASIC TRAINING
FORT MONROE, VIRGINIA, 2010

It is tradition in all the services to have a "change of command" ceremony when the "boss" completes his or her tour of duty. The ceremony is intended to honor the outgoing commander, welcome the incoming commander, and reinforce the sense of continuity that soldiers, sailors, airmen, and marines need to feel as they perform their important duties on behalf of the nation.

At one such ceremony, I heard an incoming commander tell his sailors, "I'll provide the guidance, resources, and support you need; all I need you to do is care." I remember being impressed by such a simple but profound way of describing the relationship between leader and follower.

In the various organizations I was a part of during my career, I certainly felt when a sense of caring was present and noticed its absence when it was missing. Observing units large and small over the years, I could tell when caring became confidence. And I could see when confidence created an environment where both leaders and followers knew it was not just acceptable but *expected* to challenge each other and existing policies, provided one did so for the good of all and the success of the organization.

When I became the commander of the Army's Training and Doctrine Command (TRADOC) in 2008, the strain of five years at war was beginning to be felt across the Army. One of TRADOC's responsibilities is to recruit and provide initial military training for all new soldiers—that is, to convince young men and women across the country to leave civilian life and enlist in the Army, then to put them through months of basic training before sending them into the regular Army.

Between 2003 and 2008, we had increased the size of the active-duty Army from 490,000 to 525,000, and we were on track to increase it to 565,000 by 2011. To put this in perspective, we had to find approximately 120,000 qualified young men and women each year and process them through their initial military training. It's hard to overstate the challenge of accomplishing that task at that pace. It strained housing facilities, training infrastructure, and, most of all, the people doing the training—drill sergeants.

In Army lore it is said that soldiers will forget their commander's name and their own name before they'll forget their drill sergeant's name. These men and women are feared, revered, and vitally import- ant to the continued success of the Army.

The limited number of available recruiters and drill sergeants was part of the problem we faced, but increasingly, so were their operating tempo, their self-esteem, and the pressures we were putting on their families. These were all highly qualified individuals, drawn mostly from units that had recently completed a tour of duty in Iraq or Afghanistan. The tour of duty as a recruiter or drill sergeant was to be in part their "down time" before their next deployment. Except that it wasn't down time at all—it was intense. And with all of the focus on those in Iraq and Afghanistan, even these seasoned professionals were beginning to feel like no one cared.

I knew that the first thing I had to do was better understand the problem. So I dispatched my command sergeant major, David Bruner, to assess the situation across the twenty-two training brigades of TRADOC. He soon confirmed that morale was especially low among drill sergeants and their families and that performance was slipping in places.

He reported that we urgently needed much greater focus on the challenge of getting so many new recruits through training. He also suggested that we revise parts of the basic-training curriculum to make it more relevant to the ongoing conflicts, more transferable to other kinds of conflicts we might face in the future, and more interesting to the generation of youngsters we were recruiting. I knew this would be a big, important project that would have to overcome significant bureaucratic inertia. The very thought of changing anything to do with basic training has always generated avalanches of emotion and opinion in an Army where basic training is the one common experience shared by all. I could almost hear the voices: "If it ain't broke, don't fix it!"

So I asked the Chief of Staff of the Army, General George Casey, to authorize me to establish a new organization, commanded by a three-star general, whose sole function would be to ensure the quality of training for new recruits. He readily agreed and asked whom I had in mind to lead it. I told him I wanted then–Major General Mark Hertling, who had recently completed a very successful tour of duty as a division commander in Iraq.

"Why Mark Hertling?" he asked. "Is it because of his time with you in Iraq?"

"His combat credentials with me and more recently with his own division in Iraq are of course part of the reason, sir," I responded. "But it's mostly because of his well-earned reputation for leading with his heart. We need to make some fundamental changes in basic training. Those changes would be hard enough on their own, but they'll be especially hard at a time when our drill sergeants have a morale problem. Mark has terrific instincts about addressing issues related to morale, cohesion, and caring, and he's not afraid to break a little china when he sees that things don't make sense or aren't being done properly. He's the one guy I know who can implement change and make people feel good about it." I also knew he had a terrific wife at his side, Sue, who would put her shoulder to the task and help make sure we accounted for the concerns of the drill sergeants' families.

"Okay," General Casey said, "we'll get him on orders right away."

Mark Hertling was promoted to lieutenant general and appointed deputy commanding general for initial military training in September 2009. Once in the job, Mark quickly learned that over the course of the wars in Iraq and Afghanistan, service as a drill sergeant had been disparaged, even discouraged in some cases. As he described it, anything away from the battlefield was often considered a waste of time in an NCO's career.

Even worse, he discovered that we weren't getting support from leaders in combat units when their NCOs were selected for duty as drill sergeants. Commanders and their command sergeants major often argued that they had "more important" missions and arranged for their NCOs to be deleted from orders to drill sergeant school. When Mark stepped into his new role, there was a staggering 25 percent no-show rate to drill sergeant school. That translated into a shortage of drill sergeants, which in turn meant more work for the ones who were on the job.

Mark began extensive outreach to the Army's senior leaders to educate them on the long-term consequences of not investing in initial military training and to ask their help in ensuring that those selected for this important duty reported on time. They responded to his obvious passion for the mission—and the strength of his arguments—and before long the no-show rate was cut in half.

"Cycle break" was a time, between basic-training courses, intended for drill sergeants to take care of themselves and their families. Mark discovered that it had been encroached upon by other requirements to the point that it almost didn't exist. He instructed his team to make protecting drill sergeants' cycle break a top priority.

Mark was on the road constantly, making sure that he took the pulse of his twenty-two training units spread out across the country. Often Sue would accompany him, and they would convene drill sergeant family forums as a way of staying in touch with the community that they led and served.

Besides relieving the pressure on drill sergeants, Mark made them feel better about their jobs. He gave them a voice and challenged them to be a little rebellious in improving the quality of our recruits' training. He gave them the freedom to revise the Army's "Warrior Tasks and Battle Drills," the instruction manual for turning a civilian into a soldier. He allowed them to bring greater realism to rifle marksmanship and combatives training. He challenged them to restore the emphasis on values instruction, add greater realism to first-aid training, and create opportunities for young soldiers to appreciate the importance of cultural awareness in our deployments across the globe. He worked with them to introduce the idea that every soldier is a "soldier-athlete." As part of that initiative, he championed changes in physical readiness training and the concept of "fueling the soldier" by introducing performance nutrition into Army dining facilities. His goal was to make recruits both better soldiers and better citizens. He succeeded.

It wasn't easy, and it took time. Resources were strained after the 2008 recession, and there were some in the Army—senior military and civilian leaders—who were trying to manage other priorities and didn't appreciate Mark's impassioned efforts on behalf of his drill sergeants. A couple of years later, when he was being considered for his next job, Mark was criticized by some senior Army leaders for being a bit too rebellious.

From the start of his efforts to rethink and adapt basic training, Mark knew he was taking some risk by being so outspoken and aggressive, but that never deterred him. He stayed focused on the goals at hand regardless of the potential personal cost. Eventually he attained another three-star position as the commanding general of U.S. Army Europe. It was a very good job, and he performed exceptionally well there, as he had at TRADOC. He was never selected for a four-star position; he retired in December 2012, following his tour in Europe. But in the end, if we were to go back and ask those who mattered most—the drill sergeants—about Mark's impact while assigned to TRADOC, I know we'd find that they recognized and deeply appreciated his commitment to the basic training mission and to them.

A good litmus test for whether rebelliousness is responsible should include whether it is selfless or self-serving, inclusive or exclusive, transparent or opaque, and whether it is needed to improve some unproductive process or is just change for change's sake. Mark Hertling passed the litmus test of *responsible rebelliousness* with flying colors.

ESCAPE FROM THE NATIONAL TRAINING CENTER
FORT IRWIN, CALIFORNIA, 1997

I was sitting in the turret of my Bradley Fighting Vehicle, looking out over the central corridor of the Army's National Training Center. It was a mid-October morning, dawn was just breaking, and it was an impressive sight. Back in the 1980s, some truly visionary leaders, with the support of Congress, decided to turn this 1,300-square-mile section of the Mojave Desert just south of Death Valley into a place where brigade-sized units—thousands of soldiers and hundreds of vehicles—could conduct simulated battles. There is no place like it in the United States and very few in the world. Later they stationed a professional opposing force here, so that the "enemy" would have the advantage in training events. Later still, they placed video cameras and listening devices throughout the training area so every action could be recorded and replayed during after-action reviews. The National Training Center is a national treasure. It is a key component in keeping us the best-trained and best-led military on the planet.

On this particular morning, in this particular spot, it was also where the troopers of the 3rd Cavalry Regiment—the "Brave Rifles"— were about to attack the opposing force, who had established a defensive position just beyond a ridgeline to our west.

I had been in command of the regiment for a little more than a year. These training events at the National Training Center are so important to the readiness of the thirty-plus brigade-sized units in the Army that we had been preparing for this moment most of that year. We were as ready as we possibly could be, but I knew we would still learn from the exercise, because this was the only place where we could spread out the unit and see what it could do.

I heard someone climbing up on my vehicle. It was my operations officer, Major Paul Funk.

"Brave Rifles, sir," he said. It was the standard greeting rendered by members of the unit when addressing someone senior.

"Veterans, Paul," I replied, the standard answer. "All in order?"

"For the most part, sir. As you know, Third Squadron will lead in the attack, with First Squadron following, until we identify where we want to penetrate the enemy's defense. We've had a little trouble overnight tucking the artillery in behind Third Squadron, and there's still a bit of a traffic jam back there, but we'll get it sorted out before it's time to move."

"Okay. I can hear scout helicopters making their way to the flanks. Any reports from them yet?"

"No, sir. Not yet." Paul handed me a cup of coffee. He was a bright young major, very humble. The troops loved him. He would go on the become a four-star general and commander of TRADOC.

"Thanks, Paul," I said. "You know, if it weren't so damn hot out here and so far away from absolutely everything, I'd like to be stationed here. No better place to train than here."

"You're right about that."

About that time, the driver came over the intercom to tell me that one of the vehicle warning lights had just illuminated.

Perfect timing, I thought to myself.

"Looks like you're going to have some company in your Bradley, Paul. This one just went down. I'm going to have to jump vehicles."

"No worries, sir. We better get moving, though. It's almost showtime. I'll get on the radio and get a mechanic over here too."

My vehicle would never make it into the battle. It would remain inoperable for the rest of the day, thanks to an electrical problem of some kind.

As we hustled over to the other Bradley, parked about fifty meters away, I thought about how maintenance was such a critical factor for operations in the desert. Those stationed at Fort Irwin had a saying: "Everything is just harder in the desert." They were right.

The desert was particularly hard on the fleet of vehicles permanently placed out there for the use of training units. When a unit arrived for training, they drew the combat and support vehicles they needed from a large storage lot. When they were finished training, they repaired the vehicles, cleaned them, and returned them to the lot. Both the draw and the return were supervised by civilian mechanics, many of them former military, under contract with the Department of the Army. One of the tests of units that came to the National Training Center was how quickly their borrowed vehicles passed inspection and were accepted back into storage by the civilian contractors. None of us were looking forward to that part. It was always difficult.

Soon the attack began. The opposing force had some tank crews who were particularly good at MILES gunnery—the military equivalent of laser tag—and they chewed us up pretty good in the early part of the battle. Eventually, thanks to deft employment of smoke by our artillery, some tremendous work by our engineers in dismantling the enemy's obstacles, and the overwhelming firepower we brought to bear with our tanks and Apache helicopters, we prevailed. It was a good fight. In many ways I hated to see it end. This was our last battle, and I knew it would be my last and by far best major training event as commander of the regiment.

The next day we had our final after-action review. The take-home packet from it would guide our training for the next year. Now all that remained was to turn in our borrowed equipment.

We were well organized for the task. The regimental executive officer had set up a command center to track the progress of inspecting, cleaning, repairing, and turning in the approximately three hundred tracked vehicles and two hundred wheeled vehicles we had been using.

We had allocated five days for the task—standard for units of our size. To move the cavalry troopers and their personal gear back to Fort Carson, Colorado, we had contracted with charter aircraft and buses to take us to the airport on day six.

Days one and two went well. We were able to get about 45 percent of our equipment accepted back into storage, so we were a little ahead of schedule.

Because it was October, the desert was hot during the day and cold at night. The troopers were working hard under harsh conditions, around the clock, to get each vehicle through the gauntlet of inspectors and into the storage lot. They had been away from home for a month, so motivating them to get the job done wasn't difficult—initially.

On day three we hit an unexpected wall.

We barely got anything accepted into the storage lot that day. Our crews began complaining that inspectors were "moving the goal posts" by coming back to reinspect vehicles that had been repaired and finding new faults. Our mechanics began complaining that they couldn't get the repair parts they needed. Even the standard of cleanliness required for turning in vehicles—already incredibly high—seemed to have been raised. Things began to grind to a halt.

I met with my executive officer to try to figure out what was going on.

"Sir," he said, "I don't know for sure, but something's going on with the contractor. We started out working cooperatively together to get our equipment accepted back by them, but just in the last day their attitudes changed. Now every interaction with them feels confrontational."

"Are our crews and mechanics being professional toward them?" I asked.

"Absolutely, sir. I've had to have a talk with one of the troop commanders who got a little heated with one of the inspectors, but other than that one incident, we're clean."

"How can I help?"

"Well, sir, the project manager isn't here this week or I'd have you speak with him. I've been working with his number two, and he's been straight with me. It would probably help if you had a meeting with our senior leaders to make sure they stay motivated. We've got two more days left, and we need to stay positive if we're going to get out of here on time."

"I'll do that."

"One more thing, sir, and I hesitate to bring it up. We may need to consider slipping our scheduled airplanes and buses to the right. I'm not confident we're going to get everything turned in on time." *Slipping to the right* was military jargon for moving something later on the calendar. "We'll have to let the transportation folks know not later than midnight on day four if we're going to make any changes to our departure schedule."

"How far to the right?" I asked.

"That's the problem, sir. I don't know."

"Okay, I'll think on that overnight. Can't do anything about it tonight."

That night I talked with my command sergeant major, the senior enlisted soldier in the regiment. Command sergeants major have ways of finding out things that no one else seems to be able to. I asked him to talk to the contract inspectors—some of whom he knew—and find out what was really going on.

Midmorning the next day, he returned.

"Sir," he began, "I'm pretty sure I've figured it out. It ain't good, and you're not going to be happy."

"What's up?"

"The contractor has run out of parts. Because it's the beginning of the fiscal year, their stocks were low to begin with, and now they're out of most of the things we need."

The Army's fiscal year runs from October 1 through September 30. It's not uncommon for organizations within the Army to begin running out of money near the end of the fiscal year and defer purchases until the beginning of the new one. That affects both military units and contractors paid by the military.

"Well, when the hell do they think they'll have the repair parts?" I growled.

"That's the thing. They don't know, sir. There's a new supply-chain concept they're calling 'Just in Time Logistics.' First time I've heard of it, and by the way, it doesn't seem 'just in time' to me."

"Any suggestions, Sergeant Major?"

"I say we just park 'em, lock 'em, and walk. It's not our fault that the system can't produce the parts, and our troopers have worked their tails off for the last month. They want to go home."

"Will the contractors admit that this is their problem, not ours?"

"You're kidding, right, sir? They're not going to throw themselves under the bus."

"Okay, Sergeant Major. Let's bring in the squadron commanders and command sergeants major tonight for a meeting, and we'll figure this thing out."

I knew I couldn't get any advice from anyone above me. The standard line in the order sending us to the National Training Center was that "the mission is complete when all equipment is repaired, cleaned, and returned to the holding area." Orders is orders, as the saying goes.

I also knew that there was a ten-day gap between when we were scheduled to leave and when the next unit would arrive. So there was no sense of urgency about getting us out of Fort Irwin and probably wouldn't be for about a week. It wasn't looking good for us.

This isn't any way to treat my young troopers, I thought. And in that moment, I knew what we'd do.

Several hours later, the squadron commanders and their command sergeants major walked into my makeshift conference room. They looked tired and frustrated. It was the end of day four, and only 60 percent of our equipment had been accepted. They knew there was no way we would reach 100 percent by the end of the next day.

"Gentlemen," I began, "we have one more day to complete the turn-in of our equipment. We need a big push tomorrow. I mean an all-out, honest effort to get our stuff accepted." I paused. "However, we all know that we're not going to get everything accepted. So, by fifteen hundred hours tomorrow, I want you to bring me a list of any equipment that won't be accepted by the end of the day with a brief explanation of why we couldn't get it done. Any questions so far?"

There were none. I turned to the executive officer.

"XO, I need you to find a place where we can park any vehicles that haven't passed the inspection and let us know where it's located. The closer to our current location the better. For the rest of you, beginning at fifteen hundred, I want all of those vehicles moved to that location."

I turned to one of the command sergeants major.

"Sergeant Major, work with the senior noncommissioned officers and develop a guard force to stay behind and guard those vehicles. I'll want one officer and one senior noncommissioned officer to stay with the guard force. See if you can get volunteers with the expectation that they'll be here for about another week."

"Got it, sir," he said.

I turned back to the group. "I've been in touch with our rear detachment at Fort Carson, and LTC Dave Teeples is going to put together a tiger team of mechanics and drivers to come here once the required parts are on hand and do the work necessary to get this equipment turned in."

"So we're going home on schedule?" one squadron commander asked.

"Yes, we are." The energy in the room picked up noticeably. "Any other questions?" I asked. There were none. "Okay. One more thing: I don't want to hear that we've had any confrontations with the inspectors tomorrow; they're doing their jobs just like we are. We'll meet again tomorrow night to see how much work we're leaving unfinished, and to review the movement plan out of here. Thanks for your hard work and your positive attitudes. Now we need to get home safely. That's all I've got."

The next day, just after noon, I met with the senior contractor on site and explained what we were doing and why. He didn't have much to say. I also called back to Fort Carson and gave the one-star general who was there at the time the same explanation. He was supportive, but he cautioned that the three-star corps commander and four-star commander of Forces Command might not be.

He was right.

We gave it a good effort on day five, and on day six we headed home, leaving a twenty-five-man guard force to protect the approximately seventy vehicles we had not managed to get past inspection and into the contracted storage lot. I was nervous but confident about my decision.

Not long after I got home—following three days stranded in the Denver airport by a blizzard—the phone rang. It was a Sunday, so I thought it might be one of our children calling from West Point.

I picked up the phone. It was the corps commander.

"Colonel," he snapped, "what in the world were you thinking just up and leaving the NTC like that? There are people from Fort Hood to Forces Command to the Pentagon talking about what you've done. And not in a positive manner. What do you have to say for yourself?"

"Nothing for myself," I replied. "But that system out there is broken, at least the part of it we experienced. It may have been a glitch because of the time of year, or it may be systemic, but it's not working, sir. And the ones who are paying the price are the soldiers trying to do the right thing and then get home."

"Well, it's put a stain on what was a terrific training rotation for your unit, and I'm sorry for that. What's your plan to get that stuff you left behind completed?"

I explained.

"Okay. Let me know when it's all sorted out. And I'd like you to send me a memorandum explaining what happened so I can see if there's something we can do about it. That's all I've got for now."

"Yes, sir." I wasn't sure what to make of the phone call, but I was glad to have it behind me.

Over the next few weeks, I spent a lot of time making sure my memorandum to the corps commander was accurate, persuasive, and unemotional. I wasn't trying to convince him that I had done the right thing. Rather, I was trying to make the case that the Army had a problem at Fort Irwin, and I was offering to be part of figuring out the solution.

Eventually—reluctantly, I suspect—the Army admitted that it had a problem with the maintenance contract at the National Training Center.

In the end, my *responsible rebelliousness* had identified and corrected a systemic flaw. And I had learned a lot from the experience.

EITHER WE'RE ALLIES OR WE'RE NOT

NATO, 2014

In my time as Chairman of the Joint Chiefs of Staff, NATO included twenty-eight European and North American nations. I sat on the NATO Military Committee with the senior military officers of each other nation, and we met three times a year. Most of the time, the meetings were highly choreographed and carefully scripted, but occasionally one would stand out in its importance.

NATO is a one-of-a-kind, multinational organization. At times we criticize other members for not contributing enough of their national budgets, but from a military perspective at least, we're happy to have these allies who will fight side by side with us when the going gets tough. To make sure we can fight side by side, we train together, attend each other's military schools, and use interoperable technology.

In 2014 NATO found itself with a political identity crisis. The nations of Northern Europe, particularly Estonia, Latvia, and Lithuania, and the nations of Eastern Europe, especially Poland and Hungary, were increasingly worried about a revanchist Russia. They had good reason to be. Russia had recently annexed Crimea. It was the catalyst for and an active participant in a conflict in eastern Ukraine that threatened to tear that country apart. And it was conducting military exercises on its borders and instigating incidents in the air and at sea unseen since the Cold War.

Meanwhile, the nations of Southern Europe, particularly Greece, Italy, and Spain, were increasingly worried about the spillover effects of the conflicts in the Middle East and North Africa. Massive numbers of refugees were seeking a safe haven in Southern Europe, creating an enormous burden on our southern NATO allies.

For their part, England and the nations of Central Europe, including France and Germany, though concerned about both Russia and refugees, were more or less content with the status quo in Europe. The French were actively combating terrorism in North Africa, and both England and Germany were part of the NATO coalition in Afghanistan, but the political leaders of these three countries were most keenly interested in how NATO could be made more efficient, reducing the burden of defense on their budgets.

When the NATO Military Committee met in Brussels in May of 2014, one of our goals was to consider whether NATO's Strategic Concept, an assessment of the threats facing the alliance, remained valid. The existing document was laser-focused on terrorism and made almost no mention of other threats. It also argued that, if we were smart, we could have the same level of security at a lower cost. But much had changed since it had been written just two years earlier.

Coming out of this meeting, it would be important to find a way to reassure our allies who saw Russia as their greatest threat, support those who believed terrorism and the flow of refugees were their greatest threats, and persuade the more "cost-conscious" NATO members that the time had come to persuade our civilian leaders to *increase* defense spending, not decrease it. If we didn't provide candid military advice, the concept would remain unchanged, and we would lose the chance to adapt to our changing environment for at least another year. Change is hard anywhere; it is especially hard in multinational alliances.

There is no template to define the relationship between military leaders and their elected civilian counterparts across NATO. Some, like me, were apolitical and served for a specified period of time regardless of whether the government changed hands. Other military leaders were political appointees who served particular parties or individuals and were expected to be loyal to them. Until recently, one was actually elected into the position. As a result, in conversations with my fellow chiefs of defense, I was sometimes uncertain whether I was hearing sound, objective military judgment or political talking points. Many of them knew that any deviation from the guidance they had received before coming to the meeting could cost them their jobs.

The 2014 meeting was a watershed moment for NATO's Military Committee. Amid the rapidly changing security environment, we knew we would soon be asked to give our advice to the North Atlantic Council, the body of NATO ambassadors from each nation who provide civilian oversight.

Things started off badly. Despite the efforts of the committee's very talented chairman, Danish general Knud Bartels, the first four generals and admirals called upon read from prepared statements and made political arguments in their own countries' narrow self-interest.

I was sitting next to my British counterpart, General Sir Nick Houghton, and I passed him a note: "This isn't going well. If we hope to provide any real military advice to our civilian leaders, we're going to have to stop thinking like politicians. You agree?"

He did. Shortly thereafter, I raised my hand to speak. "Gentlemen, we're not doing our job here today. It sounds like we're trying to figure out what our ambassadors on the North Atlantic Council want to hear from us, rather than figuring out what we believe is most important for our collective security."

Several heads nodded in agreement. A few were bowed, avoiding eye contact by looking intently at their notes.

"Are we allies or not?" I asked. "We know that we have to be able to do more than one thing at a time, and we need to make that clear in our advice. The ambassadors don't have to take our advice, and they may not even like it, but we get to give it to them." I turned to General

Bartels. "Chairman, I suggest we start over with the understanding that we all agree to set our talking points aside and speak frankly about the security challenges we face."

At that point, General Houghton spoke up to reinforce my points and to add his own insights into why it is so important—though sometimes uncomfortable—for this group to provide unvarnished military advice. He was very well regarded, and his intervention clearly made an impression.

The chairman then spoke for several minutes about the importance of NATO in the past and challenged us to keep it relevant for the future.

In the end, our group stepped up to the challenge. Our advice was crafted to acknowledge the changing security environment in Europe and to make the case for measures intended to both counter Russian aggression and assist our southern allies with the issues facing them from across the Mediterranean. We expressed our collective concern that defense spending was inadequate. It was a good outcome.

I took no personal risk in arguing for an expanded mission for NATO and increased defense spending. In our American system, I was encouraged to give my candid and unfiltered military advice. However, many of my counterparts took great risk. A few of them saw their tenures curtailed after this meeting, and I have no doubt that it was because they strayed from the guidance they were expected to follow.

This was my most memorable moment as a member of the NATO Military Committee, a moment when twenty-eight chiefs of defense acted both *responsibly* and, in some cases, *rebelliously* to do the right thing for the alliance.

☆ ☆ ☆ ☆

Responsible rebelliousness probably won't appear on any organizational statement of corporate values, but there should be a place for it in an organization's culture.

And there are indicators of whether it's there or not.

How do leaders respond when one of their employees says, "I don't think I'm going to do it that way"?

How do followers respond when the boss tells them, "I only want you to do it *this* way"?

The answers to those two questions are a starting point in understanding whether there's any room for responsible rebellion in an organization.

If it's true that most innovation starts with a bit of rebellion, then we should allow space for it, and we should think about how we can help our employees understand the difference between responsible and irresponsible rebelliousness.

On the other hand, as my friend Ori Brafman often points out, "no one was ever fired for failing to innovate."

If the case for *responsible rebelliousness* is a strong one, here's the compact that needs to be made between leaders and followers: leaders create safe space; those who follow take advantage of it.

CONCLUSION

I was awakened by a phone call at 4:00 A.M. It was a bitterly cold winter morning in Friedberg, Germany, and I knew the sun wouldn't come up for another three or four hours. I didn't often get calls this early in the morning, and when I did, they rarely brought good news.

Friedberg was a quaint town about forty kilometers north of Frankfurt and, since 1945, the home of the U.S. Army's 3rd Armored Division. Some of the Army's most memorable leaders and historic units had served there, but it was better known as the base where Elvis Presley served during his time in the Army from 1958 to 1960. Although it was now 1989, the man who had cut Elvis's hair during his time in Friedberg was still the base barber. As I crossed the room in the dark to reach the secure phone, I remembered that I had a haircut appointment with him later in the day.

When I picked up the phone, the duty officer on the other end informed me that the division commander wanted the brigade tactical operations center and its staff alerted, assembled, and ready to receive his orders at 7:00 A.M. I was the brigade operations officer, a major, responsible for receiving orders from the division commander and turning them into something clear, synchronized, and actionable by the five battalions in the brigade. I knew this was a test of the brigade staff, but more personally, I knew that I would be tested on my agility when faced with unexpected challenges that would be injected into the exercise along the way. We would receive our orders at 7:00 A.M. and be expected to brief our operations order back to the division commander by 3:30 P.M.

No haircut today, I thought ruefully as I hung up.

When Major General Butch Funk had taken command of the 3rd Armored Division in October 1989, we had all greeted the news with some trepidation. He had a well-earned reputation as a warrior-scholar and an uncompromising trainer. He was a Vietnam veteran and a no-nonsense product of a Montana upbringing, and we all wondered if we would be able to keep up with him.

Within days, Major General Funk had called a meeting of all the field-grade officers and sergeants major in the division at his headquarters in Frankfurt, Germany. On the appointed day, nearly three hundred of us, the senior leaders of his sixteen-thousand-person armored division, filed into a large auditorium to receive his initial guidance.

"We are one of only four tank divisions in our Army," he said. "I'm not sure where we'll be called upon to do our duty, but wherever duty calls, our job is to close with and destroy the enemy with firepower and shock effect. To do that, we have to be masters of our weapons systems and experts in making sure that nothing slows us down and complicates that job."

I looked around the room. He had everyone's attention.

"There's two things I want you to know about me," he continued. "First, I strongly believe that ***talkin' ain't fightin'***. In my career, I've heard a lot of soldiers and leaders talk a good game. I've sat through a lot of briefings and seen a lot of exceptional charts and slides describing what leaders intend to do. I don't care much for that. I'll be looking for results."

That's refreshing, I thought.

"Second," he went on, "I want leaders at every level to **take out the slack** in the processes that guide our actions."

Take out the slack, like in a rope? I wonder what he means by that. I would soon find out.

Over the course of the next several months, Major General Funk personally evaluated the ability of his six brigade commanders and their staffs to produce clear and concise orders in a series of timed, no-notice training exercises. He dramatically changed the kind of information he wanted on a weekly and monthly basis, as well as the way it was to be communicated to him. He directed that quarterly and semiannual reviews be short and focused. He was a visible, contributing presence at training events.

Better than any senior leader I knew before or since, he made it clear that he didn't expect perfection, but he did expect perfect effort. He told us that he could forgive mistakes if they were made on the field but not if they were made on the sidelines.

The training exercise that began with that 4:00 A.M. phone call went fine. We did some things well and some not so well. Major General Funk helped us map out a plan to sustain what we had done well and correct our deficiencies.

More important, *"talkin' ain't fightin'"* and *"take out the slack"* became part of our vocabulary. Those simple phrases would inform all of our future training exercises, and eventually they would stand the ultimate test when we all deployed together under Major General Funk's command to Operation Desert Storm.

In later years, as I gained rank and responsibility, I adapted Funk's two phrases into one of my own. *"No time for spectators"* became my way of communicating the need for character, determination, teamwork, and courage to solve complex problems when we encounter them.

That was true in the bipolar, baby-boomer, predigital world of 1989, and it's even more true today.

As we navigate through life, we often have the opportunity to make small impacts on people's lives, and every once in a while, if we're really lucky, we might have an opportunity to make a big impact. *No Time for Spectators* argues that we should be alert for and take advantage of these opportunities when they present themselves.

The morning after I took command of Task Force Old Ironsides in July 2003, I told the MPs assigned to transport and protect me that I wanted to visit four or five forward operating bases across Baghdad to get a feel for how we were doing. They prepared the three armored HUM-MWVs, and I took my place in the passenger seat of the middle one.

New to the job, I wanted to know who was escorting me, so I turned to the driver and asked him to tell me something about himself.

"Mike Garrett, sir. I'm from Pittsburg, Pennsylvania," he replied.

I turned around to make eye contact with the communications sergeant who sat behind me tending to the radios.

"Dwayne Hopkins, sir. I'm from Cleveland, Ohio."

I turned back around to face forward. There was one more soldier in the vehicle: the turret gunner, standing between me and the driver and manning the machine gun mounted on top of the vehicle. All I could see was the gunner's two legs next to me. I slapped the leg closest to me.

"And what's your name, soldier?" I yelled up at the torso above.

"Amanda, sir." She looked down at me, her hands on the machine gun.

"Amanda?" I said. I'd been away from the Army for nearly five years in staff positions, and I had forgotten that the military police branch had been opened to women in the interim. "Well, Amanda, do you know how to use that machine gun?"

"You bet your ass I do, sir," she replied.

"Actually, Amanda," I said, "that's exactly what I'm about to do when we drive out that gate."

The crew laughed, and a few moments later we were on our way.

That moment was seared into my memory, so ten years later, in early 2013, when Secretary of Defense Leon Panetta asked me to discuss with the Joint Chiefs rescinding the ground combat exclusion policy for women, I was ready to do so. In fact, the Joint Chiefs and I had already been discussing the combat exclusion policy for about a year. We knew it was an anachronism, but we had recently been through significant change with the repeal of "don't ask, don't tell," and we wanted to be sure we prepared the force for any further change.

The combat exclusion policy for women dated back to 1948. It prohibited women from serving in units that expected to see combat. In 1994 it was revised by Secretary of Defense Les Aspin to open aviation units to women, but it continued to exclude women from units "in proximity to ground combat."

By 2013 that had long been recognized as a meaningless distinction. As my experience with Amanda attested, women were in direct ground combat and had been for a long time.

The Joint Chiefs (Generals Amos, Odierno, Welsh, and Grass and Admirals Winnefeld and Greenert) serving with me at that time understood this. None of us questioned whether women were serving in harm's way and, therefore, in ground combat. We also knew that if the combat exclusion policy was rescinded, we would need to consider opening all branches to women, including traditionally all-male branches like artillery, armor, infantry, and special forces. It was clear that such a decision would be controversial. Nevertheless, as a group, we agreed to recommend to Secretary Panetta that he rescind the combat exclusion policy, and on January 23, 2013, the secretary and I cosigned the document rescinding it.

With the policy rescinded, the Joint Chiefs directed a year-long study of the standards required for all military specialties that were closed to women at the time. Once we were satisfied that we had the standards right, we agreed on a single criterion to determine where men and women could serve in the all-volunteer force; if you could meet the standards, you could serve in the specialty.

In the background of our decision was the knowledge that at some point in the not-so-distant future, probably less than ten years away, demographic trends were going to make it necessary to open more opportunities to women if we intended to keep our standards for recruitment high and remain an all-volunteer force. We didn't have to address this longer-term issue on our watch, but we decided to begin to make the change beginning in 2013 rather than defer it to our successors. We didn't want to be spectators to this important issue.

At that point, with the decision made and the standards set, we turned the change over to each service to implement.

In the summer of 2019, I was in Raleigh-Durham International Airport when a young woman approached me.

"Are you General Dempsey?" she asked.

"I am," I replied. "Who are you?"

"Sir, I'm Sara Roger. I graduated from West Point in 2013."

"Nice to meet you, Sara. Where are you headed?"

"To Fort Bragg. I just graduated from Ranger School, and I'm about to take command of an artillery battery."

Ranger School is the toughest training offered in the Army—not a place for the faint of heart and only recently open to women. Only a fraction of the soldiers who enter the nine-week course make it out successfully.

"Congratulations, Sara," I said. "I'm really proud of you."

And I really was.

☆ ☆ ☆ ☆

There are a lot of memories in this book. I hope they are not too self-aggrandizing. I certainly don't mean them to be. Rather, I intend them to argue that life is a journey that must be felt to be meaningful, that it will always surprise us, and that it is an opportunity meant to be experienced by participation, not by observation. I intend them to show that history finds us, not the other way around. And since we can't know which of us history will find, we should each do all we can to prepare by living a life of character and consequence. I intend them to illustrate that we all—leaders and followers alike—have obligations to each other.

Each chapter is a piece of a puzzle, no one piece more important than another.

Because the best leaders I have known *learn to follow first*, I began with an explanation of why that's important.

I've always believed that it's not just winning, not just succeeding, that's important. It's also how we win and how we succeed. So I introduced my thoughts on why *character matters* early in the book.

Without a willingness to keep learning, we reach our limits and cede the competition of ideas to others. I argue that it's everyone's responsibility to *encourage passionate curiosity.*

Loyalty is often misunderstood as a bright line; one is either loyal or disloyal. But it's much more complicated than that. Loyalty must have limits, both loyalty up and loyalty down. I hope I've been persuasive that we all must *understand loyalty* better.

Life isn't slowing down. Quite the contrary. Information is ubiquitous in our lives, and it speeds things up. It can educate, empower, distract, trick, paralyze, or confuse us. It can highlight what binds us together or accentuate what drives us apart—unless we continually remind ourselves not to rush to judgment. I believe it best that we **don't hurry**.

There are certain moments in our lives that are clearly more import-ant than others. They are defining moments, moments that shape us, moments that we rely upon to help us make the big decisions. We should recognize them, remember them, and embrace them for what they provide us. We should **welcome moments of surprising clarity**.

When I visited Beijing, my Chinese counterpart showed me a wonderful lithograph of a tiger moving as though stalking something from a large stand of bamboo. He suggested that, when asked what they see in the print, most Westerners mention the bamboo forest first and then the tiger, whereas most Chinese point out the tiger first and then the forest. In fairness to my fellow Westerners, the bamboo forest makes up 95 percent of the picture. But he argued that Westerners are too focused on the big picture, while the Chinese focus on the small details that may ultimately be more important. In any case, on this I agree with him: we should in fact **sweat the small stuff**. We will be better prepared when the big stuff comes along.

I'm not sure we're skeptical enough. That wasn't a big problem until we entered what I have discussed elsewhere as the "age of the digital echo." Since around 2010, everyone, almost anywhere, stationary or on the move, has had immediate access to almost everything via their smartphone. Moreover, we can curate what we see, read, and hear to either confirm or challenge our beliefs. Most of us choose to confirm our beliefs. For that reason, I argue that we should all become a little more **sensibly skeptical**. It will lead to better decisions in everything from health to parenting to work to investments to the ballot box.

Finally, I don't think we challenge the processes that direct our lives enough. I spent forty-one years in an institution that rivals any on the planet in terms of its strict hierarchy and bureaucratic processes. Yet it also found room to allow for some *responsible rebelliousness*—under certain conditions, of course. Since most innovation starts with a bit of rebelliousness, it's worth considering how we will allow this into our own organizations.

My hope from the start has been to convince you that it's important for us all to take the time, invest the energy, and put in the effort to live a felt life.

My goal has been to convince you to get off the sidelines of life. This is *No Time for Spectators.*

ACKNOWLEDGMENTS

I've learned most of what I proffer in this book from those closest to me: From Deanie, who throughout our forty-one-year career demonstrated an uncanny ability to influence those around her, not with direct authority but with irresistible energy, commitment, and honesty. From my three children—Chris, Megan, and Caitlin—who have always lived a felt life and who exemplify character, resilience, loyalty, and courage. From my nine grandchildren—Kayla, Mackenna, Finley, Alexander, Hunter, Samuel, Luke, Braden, and David—who surprise me every day with some great discovery. I hope their passionate curiosity never fades. For them, and for everyone else's grandchildren, I hope this book contributes in some small way to how we all relate to each other.

Few have been as blessed as I have with so many extraordinary mentors and protégés. The revelation that character matters is never individual; rather, it is learned by witnessing and aspiring to imitate the behavior of the most admirable men and women around us.

Though we scattered to the four corners of the earth in June 1974, my West Point classmates continue to be an important influence in my life. Together we chose "Pride of the Corps" as our class motto, to challenge ourselves. Together we answered the challenge.

Leadership is a privilege, and it was my great privilege to lead America's sons and daughters in uniform. It was from them that I learned what we should all expect of each other. They inspired me. They continue to inspire me.

It has been an absolute joy working with my brilliant editor, Hilary Roberts. I wish her, and my terrific publisher at Missionday, Piotr Juszkiewicz, continued success.

Finally, I want to thank Duke University, the National Basketball Association, USA Basketball, and the Washington Speakers Bureau for allowing me to become part of their "family" in my second career. These values-based organizations are filled with men and women of character who understand that this is *No Time for Spectators*.

ABOUT THE AUTHOR

General Martin E. Dempsey, named one of the 100 most influential leaders in the world by *Time* magazine (2015), retired in October 2015 after 41 years of military service. He now teaches leadership and public policy as a Rubenstein Fellow at Duke University and serves as Chairman of USA Basketball.

During his time in the Army, General Dempsey commanded combat units at every level including United States Central Command, where he was responsible for securing U.S. interests in the Middle East and South Asia. He served in both Operation Desert Storm and Operation Iraqi Freedom, accumulating 42 months in combat. Between 2011 and 2015 he served as the Chief of Staff of the U.S. Army and then as the Chairman of the Joint Chiefs of Staff. As Chairman of the Joint Chiefs of Staff, General Dempsey was the senior officer in the armed forces and the principal military adviser to the president of the United States.

General Dempsey is a 1974 graduate of West Point and has master's degrees from Duke University in literature, from the Army Command & General Staff College in military science, and from the National War College in national security strategy. He also holds an honorary doctorate degree in law from the University of Notre Dame and is co-author of the best-selling leadership book *Radical Inclusion: What the Post-9/11 World Should Have Taught Us About Leadership*. In 2016 he was appointed by Queen Elizabeth II as a Knight of the British Empire. In 2019, the Association of the United States Army honored him with the George C. Marshall Award for public service.

General Dempsey and his wife, Deanie, have been married for 43 years. They have three children and nine grandchildren.